OGHENETHOJA UMUTEME

THE NONSENSE *of* WAR

A campaign for world peace

OGHENETHOJA UMUTEME

A campaign for world peace

MEMOIRS
Cirencester

Published by Memoirs

MEMOIRS
PUBLISHING

Memoirs Books
1A The Wool Market, Cirencester, Gloucestershire, GL7 2PR
info@memoirsbooks.co.uk | www.memoirspublishing.com

The Nonsense of War (c)Oghenethoja Umuteme,
First published in England, 2015

ISBN 978-1-909874-81-7

Unless otherwise indicated, Bible quotations are taken from the King James Version. Scripture quotations marked with ESV, are taken from The Holy Bible, English Standard Version® (ESV®)_Copyright © 2001 by Crossway, a publishing ministry of Good News Publishers. All rights reserved.

All rights reserved. No part of this book shall be reproduced or transmitted in any form or by any means, electronic or mechanical, including photocopying, recording, or any information storage and retrieval system, without permission in writing from the copyright owner.

Address all enquiries to the publisher; Restoration Media House Limited
+234-8101700665, +2348076190064,
Email: rmhltd.info@gmail.com

Although the author and publisher have made every effort to ensure that the information in this book was correct when going to press, we do not assume and hereby disclaim any liability to any party for any loss, damage, or disruption caused by errors or omissions, whether such errors or omissions result from negligence, accident, or any other cause.
The views expressed in this book are purely the author's.

Printed in England

DEDICATION

To all those who love peace.

CONTENTS

	Introduction	
Chapter 1	The Origin Of War	Page 1
Chapter 2	On Earth Peace	Page 20
Chapter 3	The Arguments For War	Page 30
Chapter 4	War Starts From Within	Page 48
Chapter 5	The Cost Of War	Page 58
Chapter 6	What Is The Sense In War After All?	Page 67
Chapter 7	The Fuel Of War	Page 76
Chapter 8	Victims Of War	Page 81
Chapter 9	The World Is Sinking	Page 88
Chapter 10	Gains Of Peace	Page 95
Chapter 11	How To Embrace Peace	Page 102
Chapter 12	The Bottom Line	Page 108
	Covenant Confession	Page 113
	Books by the same author	Page 114
	About the author	Page 115
	References	Page 118

INTRODUCTION

When a gunshot was fired in my neighbourhood in the city of Port Harcourt, Nigeria, some time in 2008, one would have expected the children playing outside to run for cover. Instead I heard them arguing about the kind and make of the gun that had been fired. One said it was an AK47, another said it was a GPMG (General Purpose Machine Gun).

Such is the story everywhere guns have been used to settle conflicts. One could imagine what these children would grow into – we don't need a soothsayer to tell us that the violence has just begun, unless something is done now.

Some time in 2013, I had a revelation of a hot and dry storming, rolling wind, coming from the desert and passing through lands, leading to great famine that would last for ten years all over the whole world. When I inquired what the wind from the desert was all about, I was told that it was war. This implies that a ten-year famine is about to be unleashed on Earth, and would be started by consistent war, which will originate from the desert, and most likely the Arab nations.

You may have come across news reports such as: *"The Islamist State of Iraq and Syria (ISIS) has beheaded seven men and three women, the London-based Syrian Observatory for Human Rights reported Wednesday... ISIS forces committed serious and gross human rights abuses "with an apparent systematic and widespread character,"... These include attacks directly targeting civilians and civilian infrastructure, executions and other targeted killings of civilians, abductions, rape and other forms of sexual and physical violence perpetrated against women and children. The United Nations on Thursday said ISIS has committed mass killings, kidnapped women and girls and used them as sex slaves and employed children as fighters. ... "*

War statistics reveal the victims of the conflict and crisis, cost, destruction and catastrophic mayhem which have been unleashed on the man next door, whom we call our neighbour. Many have used Ecclesiastes 3:8 to support war - *A time to love, and a time to hate; a time of war, and a time of peace.* What we just read was only saying the obvious truth of what manner of sin lives in the heart of men, and not a proof that we should engage in war. This was before the days of Jesus Christ, the Messiah the Israelites were expecting to put an end to the crisis that was befalling them. Those who support war have not understood that those who perpetrate conflicts are under the influence of the devil. The Bible says in Revelations 18:2: *And he cried mightily with a strong voice, saying, Babylon the great is fallen, is fallen, and is become the habitation of devils, and the hold of every foul spirit, and a cage of every unclean and hateful bird.* Where is Babylon in our modern-day geography? Under Nebuchadnezzar, Babylon became one of the most magnificent cities of the ancient world. How then did it become the habitation of devils?

As I put this book together, someone is already calling for war in the northern part of Nigeria. This is what they are saying:

"Many say we are behind Boko Haram. My answer is, what do you expect? We do not have economic power or intellectual power. All we have is political power and they want to take even that from us."

"We must fight and we will fight back in order to keep it. They have brought in the infidels from America and the pigs from Israel to help them but they will fail. The war has just begun, the Mujahadeen are more than ready and by Allah we shall win."

"If they don't want an ISIS in Nigeria then they must give us back the Presidency and our political power. Their soldiers are killing our warriors and our people every day but mark this: even if it takes one hundred years we will have our revenge ."

Making news as I was still writing was the CNN report of the death of a British aid worker, Alan Henning, at the hands of ISIS . According to the report, UK Prime Minister David Cameron said that the death was "absolutely abhorrent" and "unforgivable." He said further: "We must take action against it. We must find those responsible." At a ceremony at Manchester Central Mosque on Saturday, a joint statement mourning the loss of Henning was read out on behalf of mosques throughout the north of England. It said, "The killing of Alan Henning was a cowardly and criminal act of appalling brutality by a group who do not represent Islam at all and in fact are an insult to the Islamic faith."

How many police arrests have been made over civil issues lately? A watch of the DSTV Crime Channel would show that the level of hatred in society is getting out of hand. Through BBC news, CNN, Sky News, Aljazeera, etc., one could paint a picture of disorder all over the world. Recently I watched a documentary of people building underground bunkers/homes/silos on the Discovery Channel , to be used as temporary homes in the event of a disaster, and one of those expected was a nuclear explosion. It could be read from their lips that they were preparing for a devastating world war coming in the future. Where is this leading us? Can the poor, too, afford underground homes/silos, with one such owner claiming to have spent about $50 million? Discovermagazine.com reports that one man, Larry Hall, purchased a 174-foot-deep hole in the ground for $300,000 in 2008 in rural Kansas and plans to convert it to calamity-proof condos. The silo is one of 72 built across the country to deter a Soviet attack during the Cold War and once housed an Atlas F nuclear ballistic missile that could travel more than 7,000 miles. The silo's concrete walls are up to nine feet thick. A search through the internet will prove that humanity is on the brink of experiencing a catastrophic war.

This is the time for everyone to be involved in the preaching of peace, from house to house as Jesus commanded. If we don't care about peace, then we shouldn't get married and pray to give birth to children whom we haven't planned a future for. The Bible says that a good man stores up an inheritance for his children. If the world as it is now, plunged into various crisis in virtually every neighbourhood, would be a home for us to store inheritance for our dear children and those unborn, then we must wake up to the call of unity, love and peace. It must start from the home, then to the streets, and in our places of gathering. Our schools must develop a curriculum to include teaching the principles of fostering unity and eschewing war. The church must concentrate on taking hearts away from violence, and dwelling more on developing the virtues of love, peace and unity, playing down its message of wealth acquisition. The mosques must continually teach against religious violence, with sound Koranic doctrine. If we truly care about sustainable development, it would also be drummed into the ears of whoever cares to know that this is only attainable when we all lay down our arms and embrace peace and unity. Every weapon of mass destruction (WMD) should be laid to rest forever.

This reminds me of what the Bible says in Matthew

24:7: *For nation shall rise against nation, and kingdom against kingdom: and there shall be famines, and pestilences, and earthquakes, in divers places.* All these are the beginning of sorrows. But we can speak peace upon this Earth and it would be so - Luke 10:5-6: *And into whatsoever house ye enter, first say, Peace be to this house. And if the son of peace be there, your peace shall rest upon it: if not, it shall turn to you again.*

There is no other time to call for peace than now. Albert Einstein once said: *I know not with what weapons World War III will be fought, but world War IV will be fought with sticks and stones.* Why did he say this? Because after World War I, scientific invention had led to the use of nuclear weapons in World War II, So his expectation is that if ever World War III erupts, it will destroy human civilization. The survivors of World War III will have no other war to fight, if any human still remains. And if they do fight, it will be neighbours throwing stones and sticks at each other.

The gains of life are in the Word of God we receive daily. There is always time for everything under the sun, and with the passage of time, our lives will begin to experience a transformation that brings us the much-awaited peace we seek. Years have passed, and years will also come, but the fact remains that those who trust in the Lord are not moved by the news of terror that is all over the world, because we already have a foreknowledge of what the coming day would look like.

This book is set to equip us, as Christians, to understand the times, and be more dedicated to the call of God upon our lives, which include preaching the message of peace wherever we go.

Pastor Oghenethoja Umuteme
Founder/President
Christ Movement Int'l Ministries
Port Harcourt, Nigeria

CHAPTER ONE

THE ORIGIN OF WAR

The Bible says in Revelation 12:7: *And there was war in heaven.* What caused this war? Why would there be fighting in the abode of God? If war could not be prevented in Heaven, does that mean it is inevitable? I take this war as the very first war that was ever fought in Heaven and on Earth. How then did war get down to Earth? These have been the thoughts enveloping me daily. Going back to the Bible, I could find several wars which were fought, and in most cases, the victory is seen as the favour of the Lord, when those oppressed had an upper hand, and when they lost, it was seen as a punishment from the Lord.

What is war? According to the online Wikipedia: *War is an organized and often prolonged conflict that is*

CHAPTER ONE

carried out by states or non-state factors. It is generally characterised by extreme violence, social disruption and economic destruction. War should be understood as an actual, intentional and widespread armed conflict between political communities, and therefore is defined as a form of (collective) political violence or intervention. The set of techniques used by a group to carry out war is known as warfare. An absence of war is usually called peace.

Despite the series of wars that were fought in the Bible, we also read severally of how people enjoyed peace for 40 years at a stretch. Has this happened in our recent world? Has there been any peace? What are the nonsenses that make peace become a far cry from reality? Something struck my mind as I wrote these lines, and that was the fact that though war took Lot out of his home, Abraham never had cause to fight a war, and it was Abraham and his army that finally defended Lot (Genesis 14). Does this not paint a picture that the presence of war means the absence of God? If the world truly claims with all its religious practices to be paying obeisance to God, why would a sect rise up to make war in the name of religion? Is this act not an act of irrationality?

The war that broke out between Esau and Jacob in

CHAPTER ONE

the womb has taken a thorn to the peace between Israel and her neighbours. Why would this be? We have read in the Bible that God said, "Jacob have I loved, but Esau have I hated," in Romans 9:13. What brought this about? Esau grew up disobeying the instructions of God not to marry the idolatrous women, and today, the religions attributing their origin to him should learn to obey God; that would sort things out. If the descendants would claim to fight for a piece of land, and would want to reinvent history to give them the upper hand and possession to the Will of Abraham, so be it. The new Order now is the Kingdom of God, and not the inheritance of Abraham. The earlier the world get the message of Christ, the earlier we would walk into our peace, one by one, some day in the future.

Can we trace the breeding of war to the life of Adam outside the Garden of Eden? If not, why the high level of human disagreement? Could it be that Adam's life in the field made him aggressive as he tried to cope with the wild world? I believe that if man was originally aggressive, he would have challenged the serpent in the garden. The several gospels preaching love show that man wasn't created for war. Defence became inevitable

CHAPTER ONE

because cruelty has taken over man's love for the world God created for him to tend. Cain murdered Abel because he disregarded the standard of peace that God had set in place – for His favour. As long as man is not receiving the favour of God, he is going to steal from those who enjoy His favour, and in extreme cases, end their lives to acquire their wives, lands and wealth. We would see that Jesus first matured to obtain the favour of God, and then men, before stepping out to fulfil His ministry upon Earth – Luke 2:52. When people seem uninterested in the Precepts of God, there is every tendency that they will be dining with the devil.

Predators placate the wild world, and if one watches the National Geographic Wild channel, one has a feeling of the life Adam encountered after he left the garden of Eden, because even as the devil turned man against God, he would also have turned the animals against man. So the man would have also lost the control he had over animals while he named them, one by one, because of his lost glory. So it is expected that man may have had a warlike kind of life with wild animals in the field.

The fight for survival made man develop crude hunting weapons to hunt animals for self-defence and for

CHAPTER ONE

food. This made hunters as aggressive as the animals they hunted. Those who hunt lions are as aggressive as the lions. So, we would say that the hunter's aggression is a measure of the resistance he receives from his quarry, and the threat from the animal. When we take this to the world of man, we see that the foreseen resistance is the fuel of war. Then all Adam will know is that life is all about territorial control.

Time is of the essence now to make peace upon the Earth. We can bring what we have learnt from the animals' control of their colonies to the history of war the world has experienced, and it would make sense that man's quest for war is born out of living a life of distrust and cruelty. Who will stop the carnage? Man's insatiable urge to rule and oppress has led to many different kinds of warfare – guerrilla, chemical, civil, biological, nuclear, and the more global approach, like the call for strikes on ISIS locations by the international community. All these are a quest to quell the forces of wickedness that have enveloped Babylon. Many have become bloodthirsty and valiant like the vampire bat that feeds on blood. Does this mean that humans are war-hungry and bloodthirsty?

The thirst for power has led to mankind trying to

CHAPTER ONE

undermine the rule that sets peace and unity in place. According to Andre de Guillaume[i], in his book, *How to Rule the World*: *'Wielding power does you a world of good. From the moment we are born, we derive the greatest pleasure from having our will obeyed. See how parents come running whenever a child screams for food, attention, a toy (especially another's) or sweets. Children are the greatest dictators – they always get their way. Now imagine the joy if you could command like this throughout your life, the whole world rushing around to placate your inner child. It would be heaven on earth. Not only that, but in addition to peace of mind and a sense that you are a superior person, there are various other spin-off benefits that cannot be ignored: riches, the finest health care money can buy, classy women, exquisite material possessions, international travel.'*

Are these not the cause of war? The internal war that ravages the human mind is what is finally voiced as the instruments of war. If we would look at the message of Jesus - *But he that is greatest among you shall be your servant,* and would let this be, then we are on our way to enjoying long lasting peace all over the world.

Keegan[ii] said, in an interview he granted Booknotes in regard to his book *A History of Warfare*: *There are*

CHAPTER ONE

certain wicked people in the world that you can't deal with except by force. The 40,000 years of history covered by his book demonstrate what we have been discussing – people have always insisted that there is sense in every war. If we drill down into the causative agents of these wars, one would see that there are indeed, nonsenses, that wouldn't lead to war. In *A History of Warfare*, Keegan explains that war is a universal phenomenon whose form and scope is defined by the society that wages it. The question now is, what beliefs make up the society we live in? Since war only occurs in certain circumstances and is obviously fuelled by greed and oppression, wouldn't it be a welcome idea to preach the sense of unity and peace? Hasn't there been war on the home front? Haven't we seen couples fighting daily? How can these homes breed a society of peace? Haven't we seen people trying to give bribes to pave the way for them to have higher promotions or secure jobs and even contracts? Haven't we gone to the church to hear all manner of prayers designed to prove their superiority in the claim of 'who owns God'? We can go on and on, and the questions will come back to us like a furious expression of dissatisfaction.

In the story of Esau, his father Isaac told him that the

CHAPTER ONE

only way he would survive was to break the yoke of his brother from his own neck. Does this imply fighting a war? We would see the use of a weapon of war – 'sword' in Isaac's advice – Genesis 27:40: *And by thy sword shalt thou live, and shalt serve thy brother; and it shall come to pass when thou shalt have the dominion, that thou shalt break his yoke from off thy neck.* Why did this happen in the first place? It was the desire of Rebekah, and approved by God in allowing one with the love and fear of God to rule over people and administer justice rather than allowing one with a greedy hunting spirit to pierce the heart of men with his venom of disloyalty. Like Cain, did Esau considered his relationship with God? No He didn't! Rather he hated his brother all the more – Genesis 27:41: *And Esau hated Jacob because of the blessing wherewith his father blessed him: and Esau said in his heart, The days of mourning for my father are at hand; then will I slay my brother Jacob.* Esau tactically planned to eliminate his brother. Isn't this the heart of wickedness – to shed blood? I have examined why Isaac's advice went thus – because he had a similar feud with his half-brother Ishmael, and with his mother's intervention, Ishmael was sent out of the home, so he felt violence would bring back Esau's desire. Why didn't Isaac, who

CHAPTER ONE

was a custodian of the life Abraham lived with God, tell Esau the bitter truth, that he should consider his ways and become dedicated to God? Haven't many of us as Christians used this portion of the Bible as a point of reasoning to pray and command God to release our blessings? I thought about my reasoning one day and I discovered that many have vowed not to embrace peace, but would rather engage the immortal realm to get a bite of bread by force, and as they pray that God would meet them at the point of their needs, what is actually going on in their mind is that one day God would leave His throne of righteousness and holiness to come and supply their needs where they are – in the well of sin. Isn't this a mad thing to reason about? Does it make sense, even if it seems a common kind of reasoning?

How then did all the wars in the world come to be? When I read the word, 'Honorificabilitudinitatibus,[iii]' which can be translated as "the state of being able to achieve honours," used in the first quarto (1598) version of *Love's Labours Lost* by William Shakespeare, I could understand why it has been a difficult thing for mankind to achieve a state of honour with all the struggles, else why would such a long word be used to explain a state of achieving honours?

CHAPTER ONE

The process of war is against the will of God for the world. In a dream I saw an image of gold, hanging in the sky, held by two strings touching two cities in the world – America and Rome. What does this signify? Religion, Occultism, Economy and Politics. These are the powers that are disintegrating the world. The world is that head of gold, and the two strings trying to tear it apart are what we just explained.

People want peace, yet they don't know the Prince of Peace. It is only proper to seek freedom from the only one who can give it. Didn't the Jews chased out their peace with their own hands? Haven't we seen that lands that embraced Christianity are more peaceful than those which have decided to live in their own den of lions, created by their self-centred desire? Haven't we seen that the most impoverished nations of the world are those which practise barbarism? Where did the world get it wrong? Is it not because the word of Jesus in John 3:19-21 is taken in turn when He said – *And this is the condemnation, that light is come into the world, and men loved darkness rather than light, because their deeds were evil. For every one that doeth evil hateth the light, neither cometh to the light, lest his deeds should be reproved. But*

CHAPTER ONE

he that doeth truth cometh to the light, that his deeds may be made manifest, that they are wrought in God. Why then all the peace talk? Do we talk peace or receive it? Has America, which spearheads peace talks, not allowed all manner of satanic occult practices into its land? Has this also not led to the death of innocent souls, from the 9/11 sagas to the many evil atrocities parading themselves in the streets of Las Vegas, and the many crimes in Chicago, for example? Is there not much to see about the death of morality in the land as one watches the news all around the world? It is peace they want, yet they drive out peace with their hands daily. Has it been said that the suffering of the people is dependent on necessity rather than moral values? Alas! many would concur with the devil's intellectual abilities as a means to end mass deprivations and struggles for judicial recognition, but have in like manner failed to express their moral tolerability of one another.

Raph Peters[iv] wrote: *The nature of warfare never changes, only its superficial manifestations. Joshua and David, Hector and Achilles would recognize the combat that our soldiers and Marines have waged in the alleys of Somalia and Iraq. The uniforms evolve, bronze gives way*

CHAPTER ONE

to titanium, arrows may be replaced by laser-guided bombs, but the heart of the matter is still killing your enemies until any survivors surrender and do your will. Does reference to Joshua and David in the Bible prove that war is accepted, even, by God? Can we now say that war is one of the means through which God makes man to surrender to His will? As Raph says, war is about the killing of enemies. Why would man have enemies? What is the mind of God concerning this? Proverbs 16:7 say the mind of God: *When a man's ways please the Lord, he maketh even his enemies to be at peace with him.* The problem boils down to the fact that as long as many nations live outside the will of God, war will be inescapable.

While many refer to the fights of war and the dates of occurrence as the origin of war, I opine otherwise – war is from the heart. The moment a man feels a sense of insecurity, he is on the verge of hating, and when this happens, bitterness grows and the feeling of denial sets in thereby. Gradually man would begin to starve in order to save to acquire the weaponry of war. To this end, I define war as: *the act of fighting, with words and weapons, among persons disinterested in the life they are*

CHAPTER ONE

living, as a physical manifestation of an age-long inner bitterness sown in the mind; a result of discontentment felt by an individual or a group of people, as a reflection of conceived denials or oppression from whom they see as enemy to their purpose of having a fulfilling social life. Connected with this has been, and will always be, man's search for invisible powers to help annihilate their enemies. Even in Christendom, there is the likelihood of having many deflecting to the devil's camp if they perceive that God is no longer the God of war as they have thought and believed.

Now let's look at the statement of Raph above and how Joshua came into the picture of war. To do this, we would explain the definition of war I proposed above. When the children of Israel were under the rule of a Pharaoh who didn't know Joseph, he meted hardship out to them, and they had no choice but to cry unto God – Exodus 3:7-8: *And the Lord said, I have surely seen the affliction of my people which are in Egypt, and have heard their cry by reason of their taskmasters; for I know their sorrows; And I am come down to deliver them out of the hand of the Egyptians, and to bring them up out of that land unto a good land and a large, unto a land flowing*

CHAPTER ONE

with milk and honey; unto the place of the Canaanites, and the Hittites, and the Amorites, and the Perizzites, and the Hivites, and the Jebusites.

For this to happen on the Egyptian side, the economy would have to suffer, and it surely did, even to the present day, as the productive labour force was going into a land that God was giving them. It would be expected that the Egyptians would put up some resistance, which they did. And in the new land they were going into, which was already inhabited, kingdoms would have to be destabilised – and again, war was the only answer, if the Israelites were indeed to take over the land. God was giving the best of the best for His children. Would the inhabitants accept this? The war is still being fought, as many descendants of those who fled the war then have come to fight Israel.

What makes the land so attractive? Deuteronomy 8:8-9 tells us: *A land of wheat, and barley, and vines, and fig trees, and pomegranates; a land of oil olive, and honey; A land wherein thou shalt eat bread without scarceness, thou shalt not lack any thing in it; a land whose stones are iron, and out of whose hills thou mayest dig brass. When thou hast eaten and art full, then thou shalt bless the Lord thy God for the good land which he hath given*

CHAPTER ONE

thee. Many would treasure this land. And even today, the reason for many wars has been land grabbing.

So should we now accept the notion that war must happen for us to take over our inheritance? Even as the word of Christ was diffusing into the hearts of the early Christians, Saint Paul injected a statement that would make mankind not only love his neighbour as a service unto God, but also mind his spiritual neighbourhood – Ephesians 6:12: *For we wrestle not against flesh and blood, but against principalities, against powers, against the rulers of the darkness of this world, against spiritual wickedness in high places.* So, we would see that mankind would have to be alert both in the physical and the spiritual, to be able to ascertain his level of survival on Earth. This puts every man on the defensive. If we are all on the defensive, that wouldn't breed war. It is only when one group feels they have amassed the kind of weapon that would defeat the opponent that we begin to see a challenge of the status quo, the peace that has been *ab initio*. People would want more money, more lands, more power and area of jurisdiction, more wives, etc. And to make war happen, they would take these by force from their perceived enemy.

Paul further advised – Ephesians 6:13-18: 'Wherefore

CHAPTER ONE

take unto you the whole *armour of God*, that ye may be able to withstand in the evil day, and having done all, to stand. Stand therefore, having your *loins girt about* with truth, and having on the *breastplate* of righteousness; And your feet shod with the preparation of the gospel of peace; Above all, taking the *shield of faith*, wherewith ye shall be able to *quench all the fiery darts of the wicked*. And take the *helmet of salvation*, and the *sword of the Spirit*, which is the word of God: Praying always with all prayer and supplication in the Spirit, and watching thereunto with all *perseverance and supplication* for all saints.'

From what we read above, we have the words – armour, loins girt about, breastplate, shield, quench all the fiery darts of the wicked, helmet of salvation, sword of the spirit, and perseverance and supplication. All these point to defence. So it is the desire of the Lord that we put up defence, not with weapons, but with perfect understanding of the mystery behind the gospel – Ephesians 6:19: *...that I may open my mouth boldly, to make known the mystery of the gospel.* If we understand the mystery of the gospel, we can boldly preach it to many, and raise more friendly neighbours rather than enemies.

CHAPTER ONE

The question I want us to answer would be how did Solomon manage to stay without fighting war for 40 years? – 2 Chronicles 9:13-28,30: *Now the weight of gold that came to Solomon in one year was six hundred and threescore and six talents of gold; Beside that which chapmen and merchants brought. And all the kings of Arabia and governors of the country brought gold and silver to Solomon.*

And king Solomon made two hundred targets of beaten gold: six hundred shekels of beaten gold went to one target. And three hundred shields made he of beaten gold: three hundred shekels of gold went to one shield. And the king put them in the house of the forest of Lebanon. Moreover the king made a great throne of ivory, and overlaid it with pure gold. And there were six steps to the throne, with a footstool of gold, which were fastened to the throne, and stays on each side of the sitting place, and two lions standing by the stays: And twelve lions stood there on the one side and on the other upon the six steps. There was not the like made in any kingdom.

And all the drinking vessels of king Solomon were of gold, and all the vessels of the house of the forest of Lebanon were of pure gold: none were of silver; it was not any thing accounted of in the days of Solomon. For the king's ships

CHAPTER ONE

went to Tarshish with the servants of Huram: every three years once came the ships of Tarshish bringing gold, and silver, ivory, and apes, and peacocks. And king Solomon passed all the kings of the earth in riches and wisdom.

And all the kings of the earth sought the presence of Solomon, to hear his wisdom, that God had put in his heart. And they brought every man his present, vessels of silver, and vessels of gold, and raiment, harness, and spices, horses, and mules, a rate year by year.

And Solomon had four thousand stalls for horses and chariots, and twelve thousand horsemen; whom he bestowed in the chariot cities, and with the king at Jerusalem.

And he reigned over all the kings from the river even unto the land of the Philistines, and to the border of Egypt. And the king made silver in Jerusalem as stones, and cedar trees made he as the sycomore trees that are in the low plains in abundance. And they brought unto Solomon horses out of Egypt, and out of all lands. And Solomon reigned in Jerusalem over all Israel forty years.

He built alliance with all the neighbouring nations. From Jordan to Ethiopia, people admired his God-given wisdom. War causes distraction to the purpose of God in our lives, as Solomon would recall as the reason why

CHAPTER ONE

David couldn't build the temple – 1 Kings 5:2-3: *And Solomon sent to Hiram, saying, Thou knowest how that David my father could not build an house unto the name of the Lord his God for the wars which were about him on every side, until the Lord put them under the soles of his feet.*

This may have prompted him to ask God for wisdom earlier. King Solomon was so rich, yet he had peace for forty years – 1 Kings 5:4-5: *But now the Lord my God hath given me rest on every side, so that there is neither adversary nor evil occurrent. And, behold, I purpose to build an house unto the name of the Lord my God, as the Lord spake unto David my father, saying, Thy son, whom I will set upon thy throne in thy room, he shall build an house unto my name.* The peace he was experiencing was what prompted him to desire to build a house for the Lord, though this house was later brought down in the dawn of war. Such is the cost of war.

As we move over to the following chapters, we will see the reason why we should not engage in war, if we truly want to build a house for the Lord in our hearts.

CHAPTER TWO

ON EARTH PEACE

The plan of God for the Earth was re-echoed at the birth of Jesus as the Angels announced His birth in the field to the Shepherds – Luke 2:14: 'Glory to God in the highest, and *on earth peace*, good will toward men.' What drew my attention to this verse is the prophecy of unity - *on earth peace*. This implies that peace is inevitable. It has to come, if we have reasons to build our societies. Of what use is it building skyscrapers today, when we are not sure what will befall the building and its inhabitants tomorrow? We are told that those who live in glasshouses shouldn't throw stones. Haven't the most advanced nations of this world, with their scientific and technological mastery, thrown the first challenge, seeking war? With all the advanced warfare mastery of heaven,

CHAPTER TWO

has the Lord challenged the Earth to fighting? It is only admissible that our quest of greed and insatiability is responsible for all we tend to appreciate and live for here on Earth.

Callously, humans will contend even for a piece of bone which had been given to the dogs. Must one gain all? There is no gain without pain, but we have to give up yesterday if we want to let pain go today and tomorrow. There is an idiom that I learnt and lived with growing up – *let sleeping dogs lie.* There is trouble around looking for people whose necks it can hang on, but if we are careful to walk in our own path of peace, trouble will certainly go to sleep, until one wakes it up.

I have always heard people talk of political stability. What comes to my mind when I hear this is the certainty of attaining stability through politics, because politics is a function of people's desire at a particular time, and since humans live in a dynamic world, there is the tendency of rebelling with the status quo with the passage of time. Since the day the children of Israel demanded a king aside from God who would administer rule in their midst like every other nation, they have never tasted long-lasting peace. In 1 Samuel 11:11, there was already a division, and this was calmed down immediately: *And the*

CHAPTER TWO

people said unto Samuel, Who is he that said, Shall Saul reign over us? bring the men, that we may put them to death. And Saul said, There shall not a man be put to death this day: for to day the Lord hath wrought salvation in Israel.

How can the Earth experience peace? All over the world, there have been endless peace talks – from couples settling their domestic disputes and stopping children fighting to settling those of their neighbours, and society. Counsellors have grown with the tide of disagreements. The UN peace talks have yielded little, as there are still wars here and there, with the most gruesome fighting leaving many wounded and fleeing their homes. Refugee camps have grown within the last decade, and this is not stopping, as there will always be humans living like cats and dogs.

Peace comes with self-control. The first ever peace talk in the history of humans was met by deaf ears. God had spoken to Cain about the danger of the seed he was about to sow on the soil of the Earth – Genesis 4:6-7: … *And Cain was very wroth, and his countenance fell. And the Lord said unto Cain, Why art thou wroth? and why is thy countenance fallen? If thou doest well, shalt thou not be accepted? and if thou doest not well, sin lieth at the*

CHAPTER TWO

door. And unto thee shall be his desire, and thou shalt rule over him. The desire to disagree and make war is within the control of man, if only we would all learn to do well, and be accepted, rather than forcing ourselves on people. From civil wars to religious wars, one thing is common – and that is trying to get the support of people by force. When this is not going as well as expected, there is a build-up of enmity, and the brutal oppression of humans through killing, rape of women and young girls, recruiting children into the military, cannibalism, and all the ills of their terror. Closely affecting mankind is human ego, and this has led to the declaration of 'no victor, no vanquish,' to end war in some cases. Which we must do anyway if we are to live as neighbours.

Is the word of the Lord in Matthew 10:34-36 taking root? *Think not that I am come to send peace on earth: I came not to send peace, but a sword. For I am come to set a man at variance against his father, and the daughter against her mother, and the daughter in law against her mother in law. And a man's foes shall be they of his own household.* Is it that Christ was in support of violence? What did He meant by *I came not to send peace, but a sword?* Before we look for the answers, it would help to

CHAPTER TWO

read Matthew 23:23-25: *Woe unto you, scribes and Pharisees, hypocrites! for ye pay tithe of mint and anise and cummin, and have omitted the weightier matters of the law, judgment, mercy, and faith: these ought ye to have done, and not to leave the other undone. Ye blind guides, which strain at a gnat, and swallow a camel. Woe unto you, scribes and Pharisees, hypocrites! for ye make clean the outside of the cup and of the platter, but within they are full of extortion and excess.* This portion clearly explains what He meant. The word of God brings peace, and those who would accept the peace that the Word preaches will definitely be at variance with the ruling class, who live daily by oppressing others, especially the less privilege, and taking their rightful inheritance by force. Since His message is a variance with their aristocratic practices, there is the tendency of people disagreeing – some would prefer to follow the way of God, while others, for fear of losing their grounds and source of income, would want to wage a resistance, which could turn into war. A little of this may be understood from the confrontation of Paul with the damsel who brought her master much gains by deceit – Acts 16:16-24: *And it came to pass, as we went to prayer, a certain damsel possessed with a spirit of divination met*

CHAPTER TWO

us, which brought her masters much gain by soothsaying: The same followed Paul and us, and cried, saying, These men are the servants of the most high God, which shew unto us the way of salvation. And this did she many days. But Paul, being grieved, turned and said to the spirit, I command thee in the name of Jesus Christ to come out of her. And he came out the same hour.

And when her masters saw that the hope of their gains was gone, they caught Paul and Silas, and drew them into the marketplace unto the rulers, And brought them to the magistrates, saying, These men, being Jews, do exceedingly trouble our city, And teach customs, which are not lawful for us to receive, neither to observe, being Romans. And the multitude rose up together against them: and the magistrates rent off their clothes, and commanded to beat them. And when they had laid many stripes upon them, they cast them into prison, charging the jailor to keep them safely: Who, having received such a charge, thrust them into the inner prison, and made their feet fast in the stocks.

From here, we would have an understanding that the reason why people disagree is mostly related to the suppression of truth. Jesus also recognised this fact when He was with Pilate – John 18:37: *Every one that is of the*

CHAPTER TWO

truth heareth my voice. Pilate saith unto him, What is truth? And obviously the people didn't allow Pilate to wait for the answer of what truth is all about. Had he heard the truth, and known what truth meant, the much-awaited freedom the world seeks would have become a thing of the past. Pilate reported to Caesar, the world leader then, and he would have been the apostle of truth unto Rome.

How does peace come? Peace comes when there is agreement. And agreement comes when no one is aggrieved –Amos 3:3. The only way of grieving no one is by telling the bitter truth. The question is, do people accept and believe the truth? Jesus says in John 8:45: *And because I tell you the truth, ye believe me not.* In my book *The Altar in Golgotha*[v], I recounted: *Now truth is white as snow, it is the cloud of God's presence; it is the emblem of protection. Truth is perfect (1 Corinthians 13:10) and the only substance of freedom. Lie belongs to Satan (John 8:44). Deceit is of Satan. The truth is the only weapon to freedom though it is bitter, as people will say. Truth is not as palatable as lie, lie has sweet aroma, beautifully painted, distorted in reality but appeasing to the ears, then leads us gently into hell.*

CHAPTER TWO

The subject of love of truth as a solution to the world having everlasting peace is a matter of discussion even in heavenly places. The hosts of Heaven have often wondered when the world would ever experience peace. A time came when it pleased God to put an end to all this and in the days of Noah, he brought a flood upon every creation that lived on the face of the Earth, except for Noah and his household. Yet evil crept into society again. The Lord's anger may be seen in Jeremiah 7:8-9: *Behold, ye trust in lying words that cannot profit. Will ye steal, murder, and commit adultery, and swear falsely, and burn incense unto Baal, and walk after other gods whom ye know not.* Are these not the reasons and the results of war? So if the world needs peace, then we all must learn to speak the truth, always.

God has said that the heart of man is deceitful – Jeremiah 17:9. It is this deceitful nature that is gradually eroding the values of unity and togetherness that once set us apart as the prestigious people of God, here on Earth.

So, we now know that world peace would come, if the leaders would always tell those they lead the truth – from the mosque, the church, the Buddhist temples, the occult groups, the military, the government, parents, etc. If we did not corrupt figures – profit figures, offerings, tithes, populations figures, budgetary allocations, contract values, etc, we would be seeing peace as the dawn of the new day, beaming with smiles of joy. So, war is about the arithmetic of figures – and as long as we can even lie about our real age, to be able to get employment or enjoy government benefits, war will live with us.

Jesus is the only way to peace. At His persecution, two age-long enemies became friends – Luke 23:12: *And the same day Pilate and Herod were made friends together: for before they were at enmity between themselves.*

Peace comes upon us when we are able to rule over our own spirits and hold on to our anger. Proverbs 25:28 says - *He that hath no rule over his own spirit is like a city that is broken down, and without walls.* What happen when the walls of a city are broken down? Enemy invasion is inevitable, unless there is peace around. In our various villages and communal settings, houses are not fenced, yet there is relative peace amongst the people, except when they have to fight for lands for the purpose of sustenance.

The Bible says in Psalm 34:14: *Turn from evil and do*

CHAPTER TWO

good, seek peace and pursue it. It also says further in Isaiah 9:6-7, that the Messiah is the Prince of Peace and He would bring peace and justice to the world: *And he will be called a Wonderful Counsellor, mighty God, everlasting father, Prince of Peace. Of the increase of his government and peace there will be no end.* Yet the Prophet Micah in Micah 4:3 hoped for a time when God's kingdom would come and send the rain of peace upon the Earth: *They will beat their swords into plough shares, and their spears into pruning hooks. Nation will not take up sword against nation, nor will they train for war any more.* It was first in the book of Moses, in Exodus 10:13 that we first saw a warning against war - *You shall not murder.* It is not the intention of God that we should make war, after all.

CHAPTER THREE

THE ARGUMENTS FOR WAR

Many believers have used the words of Jesus in Matthew 11:12 to mean a call for war when the need arises: *And from the days of John the Baptist until now the kingdom of heaven suffereth violence, and the violent take it by force.* This is not the case. What Jesus meant is aggressive preaching of the gospel of truth and calling all to repentance. If John the Baptist were a man of war, he wouldn't be in the wilderness, withdrawing from the sight of evil. In the words of John in Matthew 3: 7-8: *But when he saw many of the Pharisees and Sadducees come to his baptism, he said unto them, O generation of vipers, who hath warned you to flee from the wrath to come? Bring forth therefore fruits meet for repentance.* This proves that

CHAPTER THREE

he was only on the side of mankind finding long-lasting peace with God. We also see severally how Jesus would withdraw from those who sought to kill Him. In speaking to Pilate, Jesus says – John 18:36: *My kingdom is not of this world: if my kingdom were of this world, then would my servants fight, that I should not be delivered to the Jews: but now is my kingdom not from hence.*

The reason for going to war is often a declaration of *Casus belli*, a Latin expression meaning "An act or event that provokes or is used to justify war[vi]." According to Evans Andrews, on the 'History' website, in the article, '6 Wars Fought for Ridiculous Reasons': *Most wars are fought over serious issues like territory, resources or political freedom, but others arise from bizarre and even comical circumstances. Over the years, armies have mobilized and blood has been shed over everything from tragic misunderstandings and perceived slights to petty border disputes and even sporting events*[vii].

With this introduction, we would now summarise the reasons given for some of the deadliest wars fought with modern weaponry of war:

- **American Civil War (1861-1865):** This is the deadliest war ever fought in the history of America, lasting for a period of four years[viii]. It is affirmed that the American Civil War was caused by various factors, but the attack of the Confederate forces around Charleston Harbour on Fort Sumter (April 12-14, 1861) has been accepted as the *casus belli*.

- **Spanish–American War (1866-1898):** From the United States point of view, the explosion and sinking of the U.S. battleship *Maine* in Havana harbour on February 15, 1898, serves as the *casus belli* for the Spanish–American War, though this explosion has been seen as a mysterious occurrence with other responsible factors suggested. This war is said to have been fought because the US wanted to have control of the Caribbean region to be able to boost its economic interests in Asia. This again points to the use of oppressive powers in war, as Spain also agreed to sell the Philippines for the sum of $20 million to the United States as part of the peace treaty[ix].

- **World War I:** This war was sparked by the assassination of Austrian Archduke Franz Ferdinand and his wife by a Bosnian Serb, Gavrilo Princip, amidst other underlying possible causes which include political, territorial and economic conflicts among the great European powers in the four decades leading up

CHAPTER THREE

to the war. Additional causes were militarism, a complex web of alliances, imperialism, and nationalism[x]. According to Dr Catriona Pennell, a senior lecturer in history, University of Exeter: *The best that can be said of German and Austrian leaders in the July crisis is that they took criminal risks with world peace*[xi]. Wouldn't this war have been averted if both nations had kept their pride in check? A statement that caught my attention as I carried out this research was that of Gerhard Hirschfeld, a professor of modern and contemporary history, University of Stuttgart: *After 25 years of domination by Kaiser Wilhelm II with his angry, autocratic and militaristic personality, his belief in the clairvoyance of all crowned heads, his disdain for diplomats and his conviction that his Germanic God had predestined him to lead his country to greatness, the 20 or so men he had appointed to decide the policy of the Reich opted for war in 1914 in what they deemed to be favourable circumstances*[12]. This is a very salient point, which I feel is still responsible for the wicked desires of humans on the face of the Earth. In certain African tribes, the promise by the gods and goddesses that a war would be won is usually enough spiritual motivation to embark on wars. The Bible also

CHAPTER THREE

contains several references to wars been fought by the Israelites at the promise of victory by God – Judges 7:7: *And the Lord said unto Gideon, By the three hundred men that lapped will I save you, and deliver the Midianites into thine hand: and let all the other people go every man unto his place.* The Midianites had sharpened their weapons of war to fight, but God's intervention on the Israeli side led to victory for Gideon and his 300 men.

- **World War II (1939-1945):** I have asked myself why the lessons of World War I never served as a deterrent to the proponents of the Second World War. History has recorded multiple *casus belli* as reasons for the war. The 'History' website has this to say: *...the Second World War was the most widespread and deadliest war in history, involving more than 30 countries and resulting in more than 50 million military and civilian deaths (with some estimates as high as 85 million dead). Sparked by Adolf Hitler's invasion of Poland in 1939, the war would drag on for six deadly years until the final Allied defeat of both Nazi Germany and Japan in 1945*[xii].

- **Six-Day War (Middle-East 1967):** According to the Encyclopaedia Britannica[xiii], this war is also called the June War or Third Arab-Israeli War. It took place from

CHAPTER THREE

June 5–10, 1967, and was the third of the Arab-Israeli wars. Israel captured the Sinai Peninsula, Gaza Strip, West Bank, Old City of Jerusalem and the Golan Heights, and these have been a major point of contention in the Arab-Israeli conflict until now. My interest in this war stems from those fought in the Bible between Israel and her neighbouring nations – especially the Philistines and Assyria. The Israeli government justified this war with a short list of *casus belli*, most important of which was the blockade of the Straits of Tiran leading into Eilat, which is Israel's only port to the Red Sea, where it receives much of its oil. So here we would see that the wars still being fought between these nations, apart from being seen as religious, have their roots in the economic wellbeing of Israel. The tension brewing between Israel and its neighbouring states over certain holy sites in Israel would mean nothing if not tied to politics, culture, religion and economy.

- **Vietnam War (1954-1975):** This war is also known as the "War Against the Americans to Save the Nation." It is a manifestation of the Cold War between the United States and the Soviet Union and their respective allies[xiv]. Some historians see the Gulf of Tonkin incident as a ruse paving way for the Vietnam War.

CHAPTER THREE

■ **The Nigerian Civil War (1967-1970):** The Nigerian Civil War could be described as caused by the pursuit of economic and political control by the major ethnic groups that make up the country. Prior to the British amalgamating the north and the southern protectorates, these ethnic groups had lived within the tenets of their own culture and administration. There were conflicts along tribal boundaries, in other to maintain territorial control. Had not the British had interest in resources that spread across the land, and wanted to have grip on the polity and economy of the people, these people would have lived as individual units, and maintain their unique interests. There is still a clamour among these tribes of secession. But this wouldn't be necessary because Nigerians have intermarried among themselves, and most people from either the north or south have given birth to offspring with the full national identity. In the name of peace, which Christianity preaches, there is really need to foster unity, and eschew discord. It is on this note that the acts of Boko Haram and various politically-masterminded conflicts should be rejected and condemned. According to Major Abubakar A. Atofarati:

The immediate cause of the civil war itself may be

CHAPTER THREE

identified as the coup and the counter coup of 1966 which altered the political equation and destroyed the fragile trust existing among the major ethnic groups. As a means of holding the country together in the last result, the country was divided into twelve states from the original four regions in May 1967. The former Eastern Region under Lt. Col. Ojukwu saw the act of the creation of states by decree "without consultation" as the last straw, and declared the Region an independent state of "Biafra". The Federal Government in Lagos saw this as an act of secession and illegal. Several meetings were held to resolve the issue peacefully without success. To avoid disintegration of the country, the central government was left with only one choice of bringing back the Region to the main fold by force[xv].

- **9/11-Triggered War on Terror:** With the attack on the former World Trade Centre in New York City, The Pentagon in Arlington, Virginia, and the intended attack on the United States Capitol in Washington, DC, a new war order was declared by the then Bush administration, tagged the 'War on Terror,' which resulted in the 2001 Afghanistan war.

CHAPTER THREE

▪ **Religious Crisis:** War instigated for religious reasons has never been the desire of God. We may see that the proponents of religious wars are those who have neglected the path of truth. For instance, a religion that allows polygamy is leading people into eternal destruction. Why? Polygamy is born out of greed and oppression. It is a means of subjecting women to untold hardship and causing their children to learn to hate as they grow, because of the continuous rancour that breeds in the home between the children of the many wives. The Bible says in Genesis 6:1-5 that the increasing number of humans lead to angels coming to take wives. The more the wives, the more evil grows, and God couldn't hold His peace, but would later lay the world to ruin. Again, any religion that would preach divorce is not talking from the heart of God. Such religion is one with the heart of war. For instance, it didn't bother King David as he murdered his soldier by sending him to the fieriest part of the war, after he had taken his wife. Why? They already have a law that allowed divorce, and as such, women were seen as mere tools of sexual satisfaction. With this kind of mindset, raping women at will is not seen as a thing of evil. Anyone who would rape a woman is worst than an animal, although even animals display

CHAPTER THREE

courtship before mating. Those who deny others their entitlements and rewards are those who breed crisis and war.

Are the reasons given above really worth the wars that claimed millions of lives and affected world economy to the tune of trillions of dollars?

For us to have a better understanding of what we have discussed above, it is necessary to have knowledge of ecological study. How do living things co-exist and interact with their environment? How do they depend on one another for the lean resources upon the face of the earth – from air to water and to land? Understanding the life of predators, seeing the reasons for the wars which have been fought ever since man stepped out of the garden of God in Eden and trying to link these tendencies to the behaviour of humans that led to war without undermining the civil characters that contributed will help us to explain the causes of war better.

All this could be seen to centre on one major fact, and that is increasing population; with scarce resources, and increasing population, there is bound to be a struggle for survival.

CHAPTER THREE

School of thoughts in support of war

- **The Utilitarianist's Perspective:** According to the Oxford Dictionary of English, Utilitarianism is 'the doctrine that an action is right in so far as it promotes happiness, and that the greatest happiness of the greatest number should be the guiding principle of conduct'. We have seen from our discussion of the *casus belli* of the wars we discussed so far that the desire to protect a nation's greed and economic interest vis-à-vis gaining political control and recognition was the trigger that the war campaigner sees as the means to have unhindered peace. Many rulers, in trying to make a name in world history, also to opt for war against their neighbours, undermining all sociological, anthropological and psychological dilemmas that the war would leave behind for the coming generation.

- **Kantian Ethics:** Immanuel Kant developed his ethical reasoning from the belief that people should not be seen as a means to an end. It has to be a thing of will. This would imply that no one should be forced to join the military to fight a war when it is believed that such a person could be killed. On the other hand, Kant's ethics are in support of going to defend he who is seen to be underarmed, and as a result the other party is using that as an advantage to unduly wage a non-reprisal war. This again supports the recent air strikes against ISIS targets from the US and other Arab nations. It also supports various peacekeeping forces that were deployed around the world to maintain peace.

- **Natural Law:** This is a philosophical school of thought also known as, *jus natural,* which holds that all humans have the right to freely exercise their emotional rights, and therefore the onus is on society to defend the helpless innocent. This would therefore be seen as a call to defend an oppressed state without cause. But even if this were upheld as a good reason to go to war, what would happen to human lives? Isn't it possible to defend the innocent by following the path of peace? According to Romans 2:15, the natural law is more of a thing of conscience, implying that the guilt of having persecuted the innocent is written in the heart: *Which shew the work of the law written in their hearts, their conscience also bearing witness, and their thoughts the mean while accusing or else excusing one another.* This would mean that the oppression of the innocent, which would eventually lead to depriving the innocent of his/her rights, and then war, is born out of the decay of morality and fear of God in society. This is already leading us to the fact that peace is possible provided the world lives to respect God, and take to heart His concern in Genesis 4: 9-10: *And the Lord said unto Cain, Where is Abel thy brother? And he said, I know not: Am I my brother's keeper? And he said, What hast thou done? the voice of thy brother's blood crieth unto me from the ground.* Taking this to heart would mean that the voice of the blood of the millions of innocents killed in war are crying to God for revenge already – Revelation 6:9-10: *And when he had opened the fifth seal, I saw under the altar the souls of them that were slain for the word of God, and for the testimony which they held: And they cried with a loud voice, saying, How long, O Lord, holy and true, dost thou not judge and avenge our blood on them that dwell on the earth.*

Jesus, in referring to this, said in Luke 11:51: *From the blood of Abel unto the blood of Zacharias, which perished between the altar and the temple: verily I say unto you, It shall be required of this generation.* Can we now say that the world will never see peace as long as more innocent people are being killed in wars and conflicts, if this is what is expected to happen, as those who killed by the sword are to die by the sword – Matthew 26:52: ... *for all they that take the sword shall perish with the sword.* A further look into what Jesus said above would also mean that defence against war should be done on the grounds of negotiating peace without the use of arms, or the use of arms as a deterrent, not to destroy, but to force the warring factions to embrace peace talks. This would mean that the earlier we embrace the path to peace, the more we have rest upon our souls.

- **Situational Ethics:** Here, it is believed that an action is permissible in certain situations. It is an avenue of excuse to uphold an immoral unethical behaviour. For instance, someone may have been seen to be acting in self-defence when killing an intruder. But the Bible preaches otherwise – Matthew 5:39-40: *But I say unto you, that ye resist not evil: but whosoever shall smite thee on thy right cheek, turn to him the other also. And if any man will sue thee at the law, and take away thy coat, let him have thy cloke also.*

Is this possible within human reasoning? This, I suppose, is why Paul advocates in Romans 3:4: ... *Let God be true and every man a liar.* Going to war on

CHAPTER THREE

situational grounds is going to leave more innocent people dead. Should we now advocate that the oppressed should flee their land without any act of defence? If this happens, wouldn't it come to a time when the entire world would be in the hands of oppressors? Can God help out? If He can, why are we not going back to Him? Does it mean that we have resented His leniency?

- **Virtue Ethics:** This ethical standard sees every behaviour from the standpoint of a virtuous person. It asks such questions as, 'what would a virtuous person have done in the same circumstances?' From the Christian view, Jesus is our standard of virtuous living, and one would adjudge from the Bible that Jesus wouldn't have supported going to war. As such, there is no reason for humans engaging one another in conflict or war. The downside of Virtue Ethics is that because it focuses on character, it may be argued that soldiers demonstrate bravery and just judgement when they stand up for the helpless. We have seen such in society when soldiers defend an innocent person from the hands of the mob. But again, what would Christ have done? He attacked the Pharisees who oppressed the widows of His days verbally with sound doctrinal

CHAPTER THREE

position, rather than opting for war. Is there any justifiable reason to go to war so far?

Jesus explained to us that the onset of war is a time when many would come to claim that they are sent from God as messiahs to save the world, and then unlike Himself, these fake Christs would recruit insurrectionaries whom they would use to foment trouble, leading to war – Mark 13:6-7: *For many shall come in my name, saying, I am Christ; and shall deceive many. And when ye shall hear of wars and rumours of wars, be ye not troubled: for such things must needs be; but the end shall not be yet.* So we would see that the religious crises happening around the word today point to the fact that indeed fake Christs have come to ruin the world and make it an unsafe place for modern civilization. The devil's timid nature has enveloped violence-sick vagrants, who have refused to be educated in Western culture and accept the beliefs of others. In their selfish, introverted attitude of inferiority complex, they have resorted to making the world the home of war tremors. The fear of domination by more qualified people has made many of these insurgents close their borders to the infiltration of more sophisticated

CHAPTER THREE

civilization, and they would vent their frustration on the women and young girls, thus depriving them of the opportunity of choosing who their spouse should be.

In making the disciples accept others, the Lord spoke to Peter – Acts 10:13-15: *And there came a voice to him, Rise, Peter; kill, and eat. But Peter said, Not so, Lord; for I have never eaten any thing that is common or unclean. And the voice spake unto him again the second time, What God hath cleansed, that call not thou common.* And with this at heart, the Gentiles were not even forced into the practice of circumcision, though Peter was accused initially, but later in the same chapter, they rejoiced together as having also won the Gentiles – Acts 11:2-3, 17-18: *And when Peter was come up to Jerusalem, they that were of the circumcision contended with him, Saying, Thou wentest in to men uncircumcised, and didst eat with them. Forasmuch then as God gave them the like gift as he did unto us, who believed on the Lord Jesus Christ; what was I, that I could withstand God? When they heard these things, they held their peace, and glorified God, saying, Then hath God also to the Gentiles granted repentance unto life.* Today we can praise the Lord with musical instruments that were not of Jewish origin, because God is indeed universal.

CHAPTER THREE

When I read of the story of Joash, Gideon's father, when Gideon brought down the Altar of Baal, I see a sense of spiritual maturity displayed in him – Judges 6:30-31: *Then the men of the city said unto Joash, Bring out thy son, that he may die: because he hath cast down the altar of Baal, and because he hath cut down the grove that was by it. And Joash said unto all that stood against him, Will ye plead for Baal? will ye save him? he that will plead for him, let him be put to death whilst it is yet morning: if he be a god, let him plead for himself, because one hath cast down his altar.* Indeed, if Baal were a god, let him defend himself. This is good advice for all those fighting religious wars. If they so trust in their god as the one they are fighting for, indeed, the same god can send thunder or so, to win his battle. I have opined that it all boils down to the greed for political power and the spirit of cannibalism. The book of Revelation 19:19 says that the devil and those who uphold him will, indeed, fight against the institution of the Kingdom of God on Earth - *And I saw the beast, and the kings of the earth, and their armies, gathered together to make war against him that sat on the horse, and against his army.* Is this not what is happening now?

CHAPTER FOUR

WAR STARTS FROM WITHIN

The book of James 4:1-2 says: *From whence come wars and fightings among you? come they not hence, even of your lusts that war in your members? Ye lust, and have not: ye kill, and desire to have, and cannot obtain: ye fight and war, yet ye have not, because ye ask not.*

The mastermind of wars is the devil, and the Bible says that he is crafty in nature. With his cunning and deceiving attributes, he enters into the hearts of humans, causing them to sow seeds of discord and malefaction among themselves. The Bible says that the devil is a liar – John 8:44: *Ye are of your father the devil, and the lusts of your father ye will do. He was a murderer from the beginning, and abode not in the truth, because there is no truth in him. When he speaketh a lie, he speaketh of his own: for he is a liar, and the father of it.* There is no war without lies. War involves acts of murdering people, many of whom are innocent. The devil started off the conflict that would result in war in the heavenly realm, and as he was thrown down to the Earth, he came with great wrath in his hand – Revelation 12:12: ... *Woe to the inhabiters of the earth and of the sea! for the devil is come down unto you, having great wrath, because he knoweth that he hath but a short time.* The wrath he came down with manifested into all kinds of weaponry and tactics of war. In Psalms 18:34 David said of his relationship with God: *He teacheth my hands to war, so that a bow of steel is broken by mine arms.* This was a temporary measure, aimed at preserving the lives of the righteous prior to the coming of the Lord. And so the first thing God did in the Old Testament was to teach people, and train them in how to defend themselves, until the birth of the New Testament, which preaches peace and unity. The prophets of old did expect this era to dawn in their time, meaning that war wasn't the solution to survival – Matthew 13:17: *For verily I say unto you, That many prophets and righteous men have desired to see those things which ye see, and have not seen them; and to hear those things which ye hear, and have not heard them.*

CHAPTER FOUR

King David once gave a clue as to how the enemy carries out his act of destruction – Psalms 10:6-10: *He hath said in his heart, I shall not be moved: for I shall never be in adversity. His mouth is full of cursing and deceit and fraud: under his tongue is mischief and vanity. He sitteth in the lurking places of the villages: in the secret places doth he murder the innocent: his eyes are privily set against the poor. He lieth in wait secretly as a lion in his den: he lieth in wait to catch the poor: he doth catch the poor, when he draweth him into his net. He croucheth, and humbleth himself, that the poor may fall by his strong ones.* The very first statement in the portion we just read says - *He hath said in his heart.* Further we would read of the character of self-esteem, believing that he would indeed succeed, through tricks of pretence before the helpless, then like a lion would devour his prey.

A good starting point for us to have an understanding of how war has crept into our homes, churches and society, would be seen from the statement of Jesus in Mark 7:21-23: *For from within, out of the heart of men, proceed evil thoughts, adulteries, fornications, murders, Thefts, covetousness, wickedness, deceit, lasciviousness, an evil eye, blasphemy, pride, foolishness: All these evil things come from within, and defile the man.*

CHAPTER FOUR

There is little proof that a person who lives with any of the habits above will not breed hatred and cause trouble wherever he/she is present. Many people who prefer war to more peaceful means have sold their hearts to the devil. Before King David started his fighting career, Goliath had been the devil's agent, tormenting the lives of many, and whole nations would fear his voice. Even when David was on the side of God, and God was working with him, we would see that he, indeed, had a life of adultery. No one who has respect for human blood would join the army to fight a war. If everyone had respect for human blood, it would be rare to have someone desiring to go to war, and then the peace we expect would come.

So if we look into that Mark 7:21-23, we just read, we see that soldiers exhibit one or more of these behaviours.

I see a new kind of war breeding already in the home front, which I call matrimonial war, as it has taken over our society in the form of increasing divorce. With the increasing number of single parents and the call to legalise gay marriage, most of the characteristics that defile the human heart will also be on the increase. All these are destroying the marriage institution. What war does is to destroy the existing institution of peace. From

CHAPTER FOUR

our earlier definition of war, we would see that whatsoever destabilises the matrimonial institution qualify as war. Gay marriage proponents have called for the liberalisation of society, and allow all manner of persons to have what they want. It can't be so. A society must live with certain rules that create a moral environment. If they preach the message of liberalisation, and want gay marriage to be legalised, then all those who are in the Psychiatric hospital for mental ailments should be released into the streets. In the days of Jesus, those with mental ailments lived among the dead – in the graveyard, so whoever is not normal, should seek to be cured or left in secluded places where they would not hurt people, or better still, among the dead.

Whether we call it terrorism, Boko Haram, insurgence, kidnapping, militancy or rebels, one thing is sure, and that is that war starts with the sowing of evil thoughts in the heart. Now that we have this understanding, we would now see how to overcome these characters and the more we would do, the more the world will experience peace:

- **Evil thoughts:** What are evil thoughts? Is there any war or crisis that does not start from evil thoughts? Are evil thoughts not the thoughts of oppression, depriving and denying others of their rights? Here is what Jesus says to this – Matthew 5:43-45: *Ye have heard that it hath been said, Thou shalt love thy neighbour, and hate thine enemy. But I say unto you, Love your enemies, bless them that curse you, do good to them that hate you, and pray for them which despitefully use you, and persecute you; That ye may be the children of your Father which is in heaven: for he maketh his sun to rise on the evil and on the good, and sendeth rain on the just and on the unjust.* If we absorb this advice, won't everyone be the child of God, which even the insurgents too are trying to be? If we truly love ourselves, and then extend it to our neighbours, would we be involved in acts that will lead to our deaths and those of our neighbours? Let's think about it.

- **Adultery and fornication:** Lasciviousness is a character that leads to adultery and fornication, and is even the cause of rape. Adultery comes from sexually insatiable greed. Humans usually have the inbuilt tendency of stealing what is meant for another, as the character of many makes them want a taste of what another would gladly invest time, money and energy on. Anyone with the habit of acquiring wealth without consideration for others will have an adulterous and fornicating mind.

- **Murders:** Humans kill for fear of losing their pride and ego. They want to be seen as being in charge of the affairs around their dwellings, and want to quickly end any act of challenge they foresee, coming. To do this, they often call for meetings and will open a debate, and through the reactions of the people, especially of those serving around them, they will begin to discover those who support their dictatorial motives, and plan to eliminate those whom they see as threats to their aim of gaining the world. Looking at religious wars, one can see that the reason why insurgents are fighting is that they see the Christian's life of religious freedom as intimidating. They still don't believe that God created humans to live freely with the mindset of love. The Christian belief of oneness takes away their thoughts of superiority, especially against their wives. Their feudal origin, which they haven't yet forgone for western civilisation, is a kingpin to the masterminding of the atrocities they commit.

- **Thefts:** There is no war without stealing. Those who steal from others are those who also harbour hatred, and want to intimidate others. These are the ones to whom Jesus referred as having evil eyes.

CHAPTER FOUR

- **Covetousness:** This is the inherent character of those who gossip, backstab, murmur and rebel. All these attitudes lead to disagreement, and then to conflict, which would lead to the use of arms. The act of covetousness is trying to control what belongs to others, and then take ownership. This act will definitely result in a reprisal attack.

- **Wickedness:** The summation of the act of deprivation is termed 'wickedness'.

- **Deceit:** The reason why many of us are lagging behind in life, and in the pursuit of what they had intended to achieve on Earth, is the act of deceit by those who envy us. In most cases, these people, after they have deceived us, will go behind and acquire what they had persuaded us not to venture into. I have heard of people complaining that a friend persuaded them not to marry a certain woman, and later the friend became the suitor. In most cases, this kind of act will breed enmity. These stories are told from one generation to the next, and one can't be surprised how this leads to hatred and then war in the years ahead.

- **Blasphemy:** This is the ultimate sin, the sin against the Holy Spirit. Isaiah 50:10-10 gives a clue to what this leads to - *Who is among you that feareth the Lord, that obeyeth the voice of his servant, that walketh in darkness, and hath no light? let him trust in the name of the Lord, and stay upon his God. Behold, all ye that kindle a fire, that compass yourselves about with sparks: walk in the light of your fire, and in the sparks that ye have kindled. This shall ye have of mine hand; ye shall lie down in sorrow.* Those who fear God, listens to His servants – Luke 16:29: *Abraham saith unto him, They have Moses and the prophets; let them hear them.* Those who fail to listen would definitely not harken to caution, and they *shall lie down in sorrow.* Blasphemy is saying words or carrying out actions against the will of God for your life, as revealed by the Holy Spirit.

- **Pride:** Proverbs 16:18 says - *Pride goeth before destruction, and an haughty spirit before a fall.* What does war bring if not destruction? Which means, drawing from what we said above as the negligence of the word of caution from God, the upheaval we have today in society is caused by pride. There is always the feeling that the one who surrenders is the weakest. It is not quite true. The act of surrendering is the act of love, and seeking peace. Proud people don't love living in society where there are harmonious relationships. Pride is a character that kills relationships. Any act that kills relationships is one that would breed war.

- **Foolishness:** In Psalm 38:5, we learnt of what foolishness can do to one's life: *My wounds stink and are corrupt because of my foolishness.* Does this paint a picture of the aftermath of war? Yes it does! The ills caused by wars are still left behind as irreparable loses. From the hospitals to the cemeteries and from the dilapidated buildings in the streets to the hanging bridges on the highway, the story is of stinking wounds left behind to remind us that war isn't the best way to resolve conflicts.

CHAPTER FIVE

THE COST OF WAR

We may have read of multi-billion dollar sums spent on war. Then there is the hope of a brokered peace, with multitudes dead, maimed for life, victors bragging in the streets and the return of arrogance and pride in every nook and cranny. Stories are told, more of the bitter experience, thus paving the way for the young to learn to hate, and with time everything will go sour again. Bygones are never bygones; the torture received by those brutalised souls is running down to heaven as the blood of Abel did. Worship of God is stopped, and people are now comforted and encouraged. The message of the church to bring hope is mostly underplayed at a time like this as survivors who have been wounded, and have lost a close relative, wonder if God is alive, and why He allowed their relatives to die.

CHAPTER FIVE

The book of Zachariah 11:1-2 gives us an indication of the cost of war - *Open thy doors, O Lebanon, that the fire may devour thy cedars. Howl, fir tree; for the cedar is fallen; because the mighty are spoiled: howl, O ye oaks of Bashan; for the forest of the vintage is come down.* We would see from the verses we just read - invasion by foreign policies, collapse of the economy, death and the taking into hostage of the mighty in the land – soldiers and the wealthy. And with this would come desolation, as many would flee their homes into refugee camps. Is this what anyone would pray for? What are we going to do to recover the multitudes of irreparable loses? Let's take a look at some figures, in monetary terms:

- The UK Ministry of Defence says that the total cost of UK military operations in Iraq from 2003 to 2009 was £8.4billion[xvi].

- Reuters puts the Iraq war costs on US at more than $2 trillion[xvii].

- On the Nigerian Civil War, Maj. Gen. Phillip Effiong's surrender speech on Radio Biafra read: *Fellow Countrymen, As you know I was asked to be the officer administering the government of this republic on the 10th of January, 1970. Since then I know some of you*

CHAPTER FIVE

have been waiting to hear a statement from me. Throughout history, injured people have had to result to arms in their self-defence where peaceful negotiations have failed. We are no exception. We took up arms because of the sense of insecurity generated in our people by the events of 1966. We have fought in defence of that cause. I am now convinced that a stop must be put to the bloodshed, which is going on as a result of the war. I am also convinced that the suffering of our people must be brought to an end. Our people are now disillusioned and those elements of the old regime who have made negotiations and reconciliation impossible have voluntarily removed themselves from our midst [xv].

On the part of the Nigerian Federal Government, in accepting the surrender speech from the Biafra end, Maj. Gen. Yakubu Gowon explained in brief terms what the war had cost the seven-year-old post independent nation:
... *The Federal Government has mounted a massive relief operations to alleviate the suffering of the people in the newly liberated areas. We are mobilizing adequate resources to provide food, shelter, and medicines for the affected population*[xv]. We can see the cost of the Nigerian war embedded in both speeches.

CHAPTER FIVE

Aside from these, we also have human death tolls in their millions. How can one grow per capita income when those who usually die during war are those who would build society? Is this not the devourer at work?

The Bible also on several occasions puts across the cost of war, and uses this as a warning to the children of Israel to desist from disobeying God, but often, such advice will fall on deaf ears, as sooner or later they will be either at the temple of Baal or Ashtoreth. A look at the Book of Lamentation would prove the fact that the cost of war, if taken to heart, would really be a deterrent factor to prevent anyone from fighting wars.

On this fact, Jesus revealed the effect of the world wars that have happened and will still be caused by man's greed, and later explained that the reason the wars haven't been lasting as intended by the devil is for the sake of the elect, the call of God, so that they would still be able to save as many souls as possible from entering into hell - Matthew 24:21-22: *For then shall be great tribulation, such as was not since the beginning of the world to this time, no, nor ever shall be. And except those days should be shortened, there should no flesh be saved: but for the elect's sake, those days shall be shortened.*

CHAPTER FIVE

The reason the devil is causing wars is to prevent souls from making heaven, as many wouldn't have repented to follow Christ – Revelation 12:12: *Woe to the inhabiters of the earth and of the sea! for the devil is come down unto you, having great wrath, because he knoweth that he hath but a short time.*

War hasn't been and will never be the best option for resolving conflicts, but with the devil's ulterior motive behind the wars, and especially the religious wars, there would be a time when people would find solace in homes build in the clouds, if science and technology would create it. In the midst of war, the answer lies in the word of the Lord Jesus – Luke 21:19-21: *In your patience possess ye your souls. And when ye shall see Jerusalem compassed with armies, then know that the desolation thereof is nigh. Then let them which are in Judaea flee to the mountains; and let them which are in the midst of it depart out; and let not them that are in the countries enter thereinto.* Jesus never advised retaliation, His counsel will always pave the way for inner peace, as long as our conscience is clear of guilt, as not being participants in the killing of innocent souls. Every one of the acts that lead to war and then the massacre of the

CHAPTER FIVE

innocent and helpless is under the leadership of the devil, and the Bible says we must flee from the devil's antics of conflicts - James 4:7-10: *Resist the devil, and he will flee from you. Draw nigh to God, and he will draw nigh to you. Cleanse your hands, ye sinners; and purify your hearts, ye double minded. Be afflicted, and mourn, and weep: let your laughter be turned to mourning, and your joy to heaviness. Humble yourselves in the sight of the Lord, and he shall lift you up.*

Yesterday is gone, today is nearly spent and tomorrow is all we have left. Forget about the past. Accept the presents as a work of fate, and put your heart into the plan for tomorrow. This way, you won't miss God. Those who appreciate and accept a more sophisticated culture to the one they have, hardly appreciate war. The desire to war is closely related to the practice of animism, as many still use charms and consult idols as their hope of victory.

The perpetrated belief by some religious groups that when they die they will be visited by seven virgins waiting to be their wives will also paint a picture of those who seek such adventure in the after-life as one fed up with life, as such would really desire to die for a course that is not handy. To be fare to that belief, I was made to

CHAPTER FIVE

understand in one of my spiritual quests that seven virgins will indeed appear to many after they have departed this Earth on their passage to the heavens, but the fact is that these virgins appear as illusions set in place by the spirits of the underworld that rule over the spiritual realm above the Earth to instigate lustful desire in the soul of the departed, as a means of creating the passion for sex in them, and once they fall for this trick, their focus on Heaven is distracted, and they won't be able to ascend higher again – they would end up in that plain of existence, and as they look further, they would see that the virgins are nowhere to be found. This is the beginning of doom for those affected souls, and they are led into a world of everlasting torment. Life is the passage of time – it is like watching the flow of water in a stream. It would be advisable for us to take to heart the truth of life, and find peace within us. Let's stop these struggles – for what to eat, clothing to wear, fame, power, women, etc.

When a super-creature deforms itself to become a lower creature, there is the tendency that the former super-creature has lost grip on the history of its origin. So it has become for many of those who chose war instead of dialogue. Haven't we seen many human colonies worshipping animals? Many have worn crowns with symbols of snakes upon them. Others have worn the face of lion as a show of the strength in the kingdom. Even in Heaven, in the vision of John as written in the book of Revelation, one of the elders still referred to Jesus as the Lion of the tribe of Judah – Revelation 5:5: *And one of the elders saith unto me, Weep not: behold, the Lion of the tribe of Judah.* Our Lord is not a lion. He is not a devourer. This misconception had continued in His time, and even today as many wait for Him to come and kill their enemies.

To correct this misconception, Jesus then asked Peter after hearing from other disciples – Matthew 16:13-18: *When Jesus came into the coasts of Caesarea Philippi, he asked his disciples, saying, Whom do men say that I the Son of man am? And they said, Some say that thou art John the Baptist: some, Elias; and others, Jeremias, or one of the prophets. He saith unto them, But whom say ye that I am? And Simon Peter answered and said, Thou art the Christ, the Son of the living God. And Jesus answered and said unto him, Blessed art thou, Simon Barjona: for flesh and blood hath not revealed it unto thee, but my Father which is in heaven. And I say also unto thee, That thou*

CHAPTER FIVE

art Peter, and upon this rock I will build my church; and the gates of hell shall not prevail against it. Peter knew who He was, and that gave him the approval of the Lord - 1 Peter 1:1-2: *Peter, an apostle of Jesus Christ, to the strangers scattered throughout Pontus, Galatia, Cappadocia, Asia, and Bithynia, Elect according to the foreknowledge of God the Father, through sanctification of the Spirit, unto obedience and sprinkling of the blood of Jesus Christ...* Even when the Lord says He has come to save the world, many believers still don't want to accept the fact that He is a God of peace. Though He thunders from Heaven, it is to set the stage for repentance. Many still see the house of God is a house of saying prayer to kill their enemies. Who will stop this? the answer lies in our hearts and conscience.

CHAPTER SIX

WHAT IS THE SENSE IN WAR AFTER ALL?

Do the following quotes from the Bible ever indicate that God supports war?

- **1 Samuel 15:3:** *Now go and strike Amalek and utterly destroy all that he has, and do not spare him; but put to death both man and woman, child and infant, ox and sheep, camel and donkey.*

- **Joshua 4:12-13:** *And the sons of Reuben and the sons of Gad and the half-tribe of Manasseh crossed over in battle array before the sons of Israel, just as Moses had spoken to them; about 40,000, equipped for war, crossed for battle before the LORD to the desert plains of Jericho.*

CHAPTER SIX

- **Numbers 31:1-2:** *Then the LORD spoke to Moses, saying, "Take full vengeance for the sons of Israel on the Midianites; afterward you will be gathered to your people."*

- **Deuteronomy 20:17:** *But you shall utterly destroy them, the Hittite and the Amorite, the Canaanite and the Perizzite, the Hivite and the Jebusite, as the LORD your God has commanded you.*

Before we draw this conclusion, lets see Deuteronomy 9:4: *Do not say in your heart when the Lord your God has driven them out before you…* This shows that God fought the battle using men in the physical while providing defence for them in the spiritual. The question to all those fighting wars is, has anyone heard from God, that He is the one sending them into war? Gideon did what every one seeking to go to war should first do – Judges 6:36-40: *And Gideon said unto God, If thou wilt save Israel by mine hand, as thou hast said, Behold, I will put a fleece of wool in the floor; and if the dew be on the fleece only, and it be dry upon all the earth beside, then shall I know that thou wilt save Israel by mine hand, as thou hast said. And it was so: for he rose up early on the morrow, and thrust the fleece together, and wringed the dew out of the*

CHAPTER SIX

fleece, a bowl full of water. And Gideon said unto God, Let not thine anger be hot against me, and I will speak but this once: let me prove, I pray thee, but this once with the fleece; let it now be dry only upon the fleece, and upon all the ground let there be dew. And God did so that night: for it was dry upon the fleece only, and there was dew on all the ground.

Again in Matthew 12:25, Jesus says: *and every city or house divided against itself shall not stand.* The cause of war is disunity; we haven't imbibed the principle of love that God expects from us. Jesus tells us that we shall be hated for His name's sake – Mark 13:13: *And ye shall be hated of all men for my name's sake: but he that shall endure unto the end, the same shall be saved.* Yet He didn't say we should fight. It is upon this that you would see many believers not willing to retaliate when religious insurgents attack them. This prophecy is older than 2000 years, which means Christ understood that the fight against believers would happen. But we have a word of hope above: *but he that shall endure unto the end, the same shall be saved.* When Pharaoh chased after the Israelites, for the singular reason of continual oppression, as the Israelites were the main labour of the Egyptian economy, wasn't this a nonsense reason to ignite conflict on the side of Egypt? God hates oppression. When the European powers in their colonialist's bid came to scramble for Africa and to share the continent amongst them, what were they expecting? Peace? It wasn't long after the Scramble for Africa before the South African Boer War erupted (1899-1902), and *by the end of the war, in 1902, about 115,000 people were living in ... camps. More significantly, some 4000 women and 16,000 children have died in them of illness* [xviii].

Today, Africa has suffered from diverse civil and intertribal wars, occasioned by several disagreements resulting from the fragmentation and amalgamation of various ethnic groups that exist in Africa. With the discovery of economic minerals came more wars. Why? The coming of the colonial imperialists and the later fragmentation and amalgamation of African tribes brought about a quest and desire for modern life, and the colonialist powers seized the opportunity to turn Africa into their farm for raw materials, which they would export into their country and process into finished goods, and would later be brought into Africa to be purchased by the high in class which the imperialists had created. The

CHAPTER SIX

gap got widened by the day, and many who were poor were finding it difficult to have a taste of the new civilized life. Around this same period, there were emerging farmlands and plantations in some parts of the world, especially the sugar cane plantation in America, and this gave birth to the slave trade. Until it was abolished, the slave trade was the most dehumanising agony that humans domiciled in Africa went through.

When I look at the nations that supported the Nigerian side during the Civil war, I see economic interest either in the sale of ammunitions, or maintaining bilateral trade agreements behind every supporting nation's flag.

I also see enmity as the main cause of conflicts. *The Economist* reported once that the Rivers State House of Assembly, Port Harcourt, Nigeria, boasted a number of cultists as Assembly members who were once student cultists, now making laws for the state that is expected to rule over normal people.[xix] Cult activities grow in an environment of enmity and this has led to various cult clashes in our higher institutions. A time came when the cult activities were even extended to secondary schools in the Niger Delta. There was a time in 2013 when the Rivers State House of Assembly made news all over the

CHAPTER SIX

world as a disoriented legislative arm of government. Does the presence of the high number of cultist in the house contribute to this? Well this is just an example of what enmity has done to the polity of nations in the world. There were stories making news during the militancy era in the Niger Delta that the creek wars were being fuelled by government cult leaders, and these boys were used to secure their position in government. The wider implication of this is that with the acquisition of armaments by individuals not licensed to carry guns, there is a possibility of an imminent war about to be unleashed on unsuspecting law-abiding citizens. The book of Ezra 4:4,5 tells us what enmity could lead to: *Then the people of the land weakened the hands of the people of Judah, and troubled them in building, And hired counsellors against them, to frustrate their purpose.*

What is the wisdom in praying if we are going to use force to achieve world peace? The Bible advices in 1 Timothy 2:1-4: *I urge, then, first of all, that requests, prayers, intercession and thanksgiving be made for everyone- for kings and all those in authority, that we may live peaceful and quiet lives in all godliness and holiness. This is good, and pleases God our Saviour, who wants all*

CHAPTER SIX

men to be saved and to come to a knowledge of the truth. We have heard of God thundering from heaven and fighting the enemy. In the land of Egypt, as God was about releasing the oppressed children of Israel, He didn't resort to war, because that would mean the death of civilians. It was only when Pharaoh chased the Israelites into the Red Sea that God went against Pharaoh and his armies. At least the destruction didn't happen where we have civilians. For those who still support the use of war to achieve world peace, or to prove superiority, the vengeance of God is too real to be ignored. The book of Revelation 8:5-7, 11:15: says of this - *And the angel took the censer, and filled it with fire of the altar, and cast it into the earth: and there were voices, and thunderings, and lightnings, and an earthquake. And the seven angels which had the seven trumpets prepared themselves to sound. The first angel sounded, and there followed hail and fire mingled with blood, and they were cast upon the earth: and the third part of trees was burnt up, and all green grass was burnt up ... And the seventh angel sounded; and there were great voices in heaven, saying, The kingdoms of this world are become the kingdoms of our Lord, and of his Christ; and he shall reign for ever and*

CHAPTER SIX

ever. Another verse of the Bible that encourages us not to take to war with our physical strength is Matthew 26:53, as Jesus explained what angels can do if we engage their services by praying to God: *Thinkest thou that I cannot now pray to my Father, and he shall presently give me more than twelve legions of angels.*

We won't take to war as heirs of the Kingdom, as long as we make our way right before the Lord. What I think is making people helpless is lack of sound doctrinal maturity on how to engage the hosts of the spiritual realm. Many that pray, pray amiss. How were the disciples freed from prisons as they went about doing the will of God? It should not be heard of us as one with bloodstains on our hands. Severally, the Bible contains examples of blood being upon people who had killed, and likewise upon their descendants – Matthew 23:35:*That upon you may come all the righteous blood shed upon the earth, from the blood of righteous Abel unto the blood of Zacharias son of Barachias, whom ye slew between the temple and the altar.* Is this what we want to happen to us? Except for the purpose of defence, and as a last resort, and provided one hears the voice of God to do that, there is no need to take life – it is the most

CHAPTER SIX

expensive of all God's creation. Once blood is spilled, it cannot be gathered. The Bible says in **Proverbs 3:5-6:** *Trust in the Lord with all thine heart; and lean not unto thine own understanding. In all thy ways acknowledge him, and he shall direct thy paths.* This is what we shall do as we continually seek Him in this trying time.

CHAPTER SEVEN

THE FUEL OF WAR

As an introductory message before we read ahead, let's see Philippians 2:4: *Look not every man on his own things, but every man also on the things of others.* Our concern is how we see others. We have asked who spilled the milk. If we have also cleaned up the mess, now what on Earth would ever cause the feud? This is what we want to discuss here. It may seem as though we are repeating the same thing over and over. It is not quite the same, but as a matter of emphasis, it is ideal to attack the same issue from different angles, to get a perfect picture of the subject under scrutiny.

The one who brought home insect-infested firewood is the one who invites lizards to a feasting context, so the saying goes. There is no fire without fuel. What does fuel do to fire? It ensures that the fire keeps burning. Three components must be present for fire to burn – fuel, oxygen and a source of ignition. In the same way, for war to happen, there must be an existing disagreement or one has to be manufactured, there must be weapons of war or the means to acquire them, and there must be humans to fight the war.

I have seen severally that withdrawal from war is not really done because the warring parties have decided to iron out their differences amicably, but as an avenue to go back and save more money to be wasted in the next round of war. God says that the heart of man is desperately wicked and He also gave their reward – Jeremiah 17:9-11:*The heart is deceitful above all things, and desperately wicked: who can know it? I the Lord search the heart, I try the reins, even to give every man according to his ways, and according to the fruit of his doings. As the partridge sitteth on eggs, and hatcheth them not; so he that getteth riches, and not by right, shall leave them in the midst of his days, and at his end shall be a fool*, and this wickedness has shown itself in the manner in which man has learnt to manufacture weapons of mass destruction.

The more we make people believe that risk-taking is a part of life, the more they will not value life. The more we would support abortions of foetuses, the more lives will not be valued. The more witch doctors demand for human parts for rituals, the more human lives will not be treasured. The more we have domestic violence in our marriages, the more we will teach our children to treat their neighbours as less than they are, and that will breed disrespect for human dignity. We have taken life as mere fate, and this has made many see life as the survival of the fittest.

The Prophet says in Isaiah 1:23: *Thy princes are rebellious, and companions of thieves: every one loveth gifts, and followeth after rewards: they judge not the fatherless, neither doth the cause of the widow come unto them.* This is the fuel of war. As long as anyone feels above persecution, takes bribes, looks only in the direction of those that favour their ill course, not willing to stand for the deprived and oppressed, a time will come when those pushed against the wall want to retaliate and set themselves free from agony. It will mean a do or die affair. But why should this be?

From the Global Peace Index criteria table, one would see the various indicators, 22 in number, used as ranking criteria for the level of peace in a nation.

CHAPTER SEVEN

This list includes:[xx]

1. Number of external and internal conflicts fought
2. Number of deaths from organised conflict (external)
3. Number of deaths from organised conflict (internal)
4. Level of organised conflict (internal)
5. Relations with neighbouring countries
6. Level of perceived criminality in society
7. Number of refugees and displaced persons as percentage of population
8. Political instability
9. Terrorist activity
10. Political Terror Scale
11. Number of homicides per 100,000 people
12. Level of violent crime
13. Likelihood of violent demonstrations
14. Number of jailed persons per 100,000 people
15. Number of internal security officers and police per 100,000 people
16. Military expenditure as a percentage of GDP
17. Number of armed services personnel

CHAPTER SEVEN

18. Volume of transfers of major conventional weapons as recipient (imports) per 100,000 people
19. Volume of transfers of major conventional weapons as supplier (exports) per 100,000 people
20. Financial contribution to UN peacekeeping missions
21. Nuclear and heavy weapons capability
22. Ease of access to small arms and light weapons

From this list we can see that various factors have been put together in an attempt to find the culprit. The fuel of war, as I said earlier, is not in the list above; it is in the breeding of enmity, which is usually sown in the heart by our parents, and stories of deprivation existing in our communities. I see this attempt, though worthy of accolades, is like 'begging the question' – *petito principi,* of what the root cause of war is.

CHAPTER EIGHT

VICTIMS OF WAR

War leads to the gross abuse of human rights and dignity. In speaking about the victims of war, as it relates to women and children, Jesus says – Mark 13:17: *But woe to them that are with child, and to them that give suck in those days.* In verses 18 and 19 he further made reference to people running and seeking refuge in other nations, and His prayer is that this should not be in the winter so that many wouldn't die of cold-related ailments - *And pray ye that your flight be not in the winter. For in those days shall be affliction, such as was not from the beginning of the creation which God created unto this time, neither shall be.* We would understand what the victims of war are, as can be seen, if we take a look at the environments where wars are fought, and what happens to whatever lives there. First, the emotional distress that envelopes those who have heard the sound of shelling will make them live in fear all the days of their lives. I don't believe that God does support deaths in multitudes. If He does, He wouldn't have reduced Gideon's soldiers from 32,000 to 300 - Judges 7:7: *And the Lord said unto Gideon, By the three hundred men that lapped will I save you.* A time came when Israel was so proud of the numbers of its soldiers as a measure of its strength that He was moved with anger against David, to number them as if trying to let them know that no matter their numbers, war is no respecter of multitudes, 1 Chronicles 21. Again we would see that at the defeat of Goliath, a stone was all He needed to bring down the insurgent devil. So God is not in support of the deaths of multitudes, which is a negation of religious beliefs that they do fight a holy war, in defence of God.

In recounting the pains of the Niger Delta Militancy era in Nigeria, in my book, 'Leadership – An Eagle Eye Perspective[xxi],' I wrote – *the militancy era in Nigeria, which lasted from 2006 to 2010. These groups claimed that they were fighting a genuine cause, and their leaders recruited more hands to help them fight the guerrilla war in the creeks of the Niger Delta.*

CHAPTER EIGHT

Soon those they were fighting for, the poor inhabitants of the dirty and oil-polluted creeks of the Delta, who had to continuously looked to God for a sip of good water only when it rained, started complaining and shouting for help. Innocent women and young girls were being raped by these now-animalized persons. It became a hunt, and the untamed politician used them to meet ends. People rushed to God to pray for this to end.

Some of the government security forces who should have helped the situation connived with these militias and started the exploitation of crude oil pipes and the scavenging of the fuel-ready condensate, which they now marketed to the public. Many lives were lost when this fake fuel went into the kerosene stoves of the same poor people, whom they had eagerly convinced the world that they were representing. Kidnapping was on the increase, children became victims and the government paid lip service to the safety of the oppressed people, in this propagandisation of a militarised hellhole. The situation was chaotic. The 'loose ends' in society, popularly called armed bandits, took to the streets with handguns to make life even more unbearable. It was as if crime was legalised, from Delta State to Cross Rivers State - the story was the

CHAPTER EIGHT

same everywhere in the oil-rich Delta. And it went into the towns of Aba, and started moving up North.

This was a locust-spreading inferno, and the pains went even deeper in the hearts of Nigerians. Those who started the fight were already losing ground too as those whom they recruited no longer obeyed them, and often broke out to start a camp of their own. There and then they realised that they had lost focus of the objective of their fight. Guns and ammunitions were in the streets. Education was decaying, and who cared? After all, there were graduates roaming the streets as hopeless, helpless and disease-prone vagrants.

Today, the city of Warri is a more desolate environment as many companies have deserted the environment, and this has heightened crimes and unemployment, with an attendant high level of prostitutions and other moral vices. No one would have thought that the several wars between the Ijaws and the Itsekiris and the upsurge of militia in the area would have led to such a level of destruction and underdevelopment. As it has now turned out, the years of oil exploration and exploitation in the area have left little good, only the wreckage that is seen in the creeks.

CHAPTER EIGHT

The quest for money has rendered many youths in the Niger Delta creek not willing to attend educational institutions. As at 2014, despite the high volume of oil pumped out of the land of the Niger Delta, the states of Rivers, Bayelsa and Cross River, are still seen as Educationally Less Developed States (ELDS), and therefore given special concessions for admissions into Nigerian universities. The fragile environment created by war has also contributed to this, and is making the situation worse. Although the governments, especially that of Rivers State, have built modern primary schools, there is still a high level of nonchalance in attitudes, especially of those in the creeks, towards accepting a refined order of life. They would rather want to still bear arms and bunker crude oil for their local improvised refineries, as a means to earning money.

As one plunges into the creeks, the story is the same. Many sit to bemoan their fate as the once busy environment, due to business and oil exploration activities, is dying by the day. It will still take a decade, if not more, before the Niger Delta would wake up from the effect of the militia-guerrilla patterned warfare that lasted for about five years.

CHAPTER EIGHT

According to Graca Machel, UN Expert on the subject and a former Minister for Education in Mozambique, from the findings she gathered in a two-year process of research and consultation, she found out that: "Millions of children are caught up in conflicts in which they are not merely bystanders, but targets. Some fall victim to a general onslaught against civilians; others die as part of a calculated genocide. Still other children suffer the effects of sexual violence or the multiple deprivations of armed conflict that expose them to hunger or disease. Just as shocking, thousands of young people are cynically exploited as combatants.[xxii]" She explains further that, "War violates every right of a child – the right to life, the right to be with family and community, the right to health, the right to the development of the personality and the right to be nurtured and protected."

UNESCO writes: *over the last decade alone, armed conflict has claimed the lives of over 2 million children. Another six million have been left wounded or disabled for life. One million have become orphans. It is estimated today that more than 300,000 children have been enrolled in militia groups and armies and been forced to carry a gun. Half of those they kill are other children*[xxiii].

CHAPTER EIGHT

From whichever angle we look at it, the deaths of children, the rape of innocent women and young girls, the maiming for life of so many others, the deaths of animals and the underlying decay to social, political and economic life would need to be looked into by warring factions, and other means devised of putting across their grievances. From the Bible we are told that war broke out in Heaven leading to the devil been thrown down to Earth, and the devil hasn't stopped claiming lives since he put his foot on Earth. We must appeal to every conscience of truth, so that our lullaby of peace will echo across the walls of grievances, and quell every disagreement caused by 'sociopoliticoreligious' indifference. Tolerance and acceptance are key if we are to live as a family.

CHAPTER NINE

THE WORLD IS SINKING

War has been fought, peace has returned, but the obvious fact remains that the Earth is becoming a desolate wasteland as the ruins of war keep multiplying. Of what use will it be celebrating a marriage union tomorrow when we are certain that soon we will fight wars, and eliminate the offspring? Of what use is it if we spend hours and use resources fashioning an engineering masterpiece, only to set it ablaze at the slightest disagreement? Or of what use is sending children to school when we are not certain if they will return back home safely to add to the joy of unity in the home? Of what use is it giving birth to a child who becomes an insurgent in society? And of what use is mining iron from the Earth, if we form it into weapons to destroy fellow

CHAPTER NINE

humans? The earlier we answer these questions the earlier we are moving in the direction of peace.

In Psalms 61:1-3, King David prayed - *O God, thou hast cast us off, thou hast scattered us, thou hast been displeased; O turn thyself to us again. Thou hast made the earth to tremble; thou hast broken it: heal the breaches thereof; for it shaketh. Thou hast shewed thy people hard things: thou hast made us to drink the wine of astonishment.* We only cast out what has been of no use to us. God wouldn't cast out what He deems useful. When I read this portion of the Bible, what came to my mind was the very fact that those cast out of God's Kingdom can never experience peace, and if many of the wars that have been fought which have been claimed by insurgents to be the defence of God were truly as claimed, then the Lord would have thundered from heaven to give them landmark victory. People make war in the name of God because they don't have any idea who God is, and what He created this world for. Gradually this world is becoming a cast-off jalopy. When God finished His creation the Bible says – Genesis 1:31: *...And God saw every thing that he had made, and, behold, it was very good.* Yet, our existence on the Earth is gradually turning it into a desolate planet.

CHAPTER NINE

Was it not in the book of Genesis 6:5-6 that we first read about an account of a world threading the path of extermination? His account of the world then was - *And God saw that the wickedness of man was great in the earth, and that every imagination of the thoughts of his heart was only evil continually. And it repented the Lord that he had made man on the earth, and it grieved him at his heart.* The Lord looked down on Earth, and what he saw couldn't take away His anger to destroy a world He had created and approved as 'very good.' Has the world changed since then? No! Rather, the world has become a mess of idolatrous worship, occult practices and tainting of the word of God for personal wealth aggrandizement desires, and the neglect of civil responsibilities.

With the development of nuclear weapons, the desolation spoken of by Daniel in the book of Daniel 8 has come to be like the sun that glares upon our faces daily. When Jack Vance, who served in the United States Merchant Marine during World War II, wrote *The Dying Earth* in 1950, he little knew that he was seeing a vision of a world which the insatiable, aggressive quest for the spilling of human blood would render desolate. The

CHAPTER NINE

experience of World War II might have ignited his prediction of what kind of forces would overrun the Earth with witchcraft and magical powers, which we see today as what science and technology has brought upon the face of the Earth, as it relates to the procreation of war ammunitions and ease of communication. The stories of the Dying Earth series are set in the distant future, at a point when the sun is almost exhausted and magic has reasserted itself as a dominant force. The Moon has disappeared and the Sun is in danger of burning out at any time, often flickering as if about to go out before shining again. The various civilizations of Earth have collapsed for the most part into decadence and its inhabitants are overcome with a fatalistic outlook. The Earth is mostly barren and cold, and has become infested with various predatory monsters[xxiv].

Is the Earth not moving gradually into a disordered state already? We must all ignite our passion for love and let our consciences speak. There is no other time to put our consciences to the test than now. Can humanity ever forgive itself for the atrocities it has unleashed upon the face of this Earth, and even far beneath the depths of the Earth with the damage done by the likes of the Hiroshima

CHAPTER NINE

atomic bomb? And the question is, ' why would Japan's Emperor Hirohito wait until a devastating bomb had hit the country before surrendering? The history.com website recalls:

On August 6, 1945, during World War II (1939-45), an American B-29 bomber dropped the world's first deployed atomic bomb over the Japanese city of Hiroshima. The explosion wiped out 90 percent of the city and immediately killed 80,000 people; tens of thousands more would later die of radiation exposure. Three days later, a second B-29 dropped another A-bomb on Nagasaki, killing an estimated 40,000 people[xxv].

The ruin of that city will forever spark hatred for the US and the world, even from generations unborn. The AtomicBombMuseum.org wrote of the Hiroshima bomb:

Of the city's 298 medical doctors, 270 (90%) became A-bomb victims. Casualty rates among pharmacists, nurses, and other medical professionals ranged between 80% and 93%. Eighteen emergency hospitals and 32 first-aid clinics were destroyed, and most of the workers needed to restore these health facilities were killed or injured. Nearby army medical facilities were also mostly destroyed[xxvi].

CHAPTER NINE

With doctors reported killed here, who would be left to care for the injured commoner in the street?

Martin J. Sherwin, a Pulitzer Prize-winning American historian, in his book, *A World Destroyed: Hiroshima and Its Legacies*, including facts he gathered from other credible sources, wrote:

... Post-war Japan chaotic. The air raids on urban centers left millions displaced and food shortages, created by bad harvests and the demands of the war, worsened when the importation of food from Korea, Taiwan, and China ceased. Repatriation of Japanese living in other parts of Asia only aggravated the problems in Japan as these displaced people put more strain on already scarce resources. Over 5.1 million Japanese returned to Japan in the fifteen months following October 1, 1945. Alcohol and drug abuse became major problems. Deep exhaustion, declining morale and despair was so widespread that it was termed the "kyodatsu condition." Inflation as rampant and many people turned to the black market for even the most basic goods. Prostitution also increased considerably[xxvii].

What do we have to say to this reality? Should we allow the world to decay further? Should we sit on the

CHAPTER NINE

fence as though we had no regard for God's creation and the world He gladly handed over to us to tender? If we truly believe in life after death, have we done all that would make God accept our souls when we depart the Earth? Too many questions that will put our conscience to work, I guess!

CHAPTER TEN

GAINS OF PEACE

Expressing concern about the proliferation of nuclear weapons, as many more nations are discovering nuclear power, the UN Secretary-General, Ban Ki-moon, 'Remarks to the Conference on Disarmament,' in Geneva (Switzerland), on the 26th January 2011, advised: *Ladies and Gentlemen, the continued deadlock has ominous implications for international security. The longer it persists, the graver the nuclear threat - from existing arsenals, from the proliferation of such weapons, and from their possible acquisition by terrorists*[xxviii].

Why should we feel resentment about ourselves and develop xenophobia towards each other, knowing that we are all intertwined in one way or the other as children of God? Usually, revolution in a country causes concerns to many people. Top among these are business owners

CHAPTER TEN

and prospective investors. It affects bilateral ties among warring nations. The gains of unity cannot be overemphasized. Peace brings along with it financial, professional, educational, and medical benefits. On the financial side, we would save the money which would have been used in procuring ammunition and servicing loans or aids that would have been borrowed from other nations. Professionals can now stay within the shores of their country and bring to bear their professional expertise in the development of the nation. This would reduce the effect of the 'brain drain' which has affected many nations that have not experienced peace in the last decade or so. Educational standards would improve, as more money would be made available to upgrade educational infrastructures that would enable the populace to learn and be educated in a conducive war-free environment. The available medical institutions in the country would be adequate for the population, as there wouldn't be new ailments resulting from war. There would also be the diversion of funds that would have been used for ammunition into building more hospitals and buying medical equipment. The government would also be able to provide free medical care for the aged, and thereby reduce the morbidity rate, sustaining the passage of history and culture from one generation to the next. The love for national development and growth would also increase as people saw the growth that came from their dedication and service in the nation. Our medical institutions would turn out more doctors, and we would then become exporters of qualified professional labour to other parts of the world. And that would mean an increase in national Gross Domestic Product (GDP), and national prestige.

Gains of peace bring hope. There would be increasing revenue from tourism and investment. Our women would be seen as good mothers within and outside, and they would be desired for marriage. We would be given ears among other nations at world conferences, and we would then stand as heralds of peace, and preachers of the gospel of truth and unity. This fact made the Prophet Micah to prophesy – Micah 4:2-4: *And many nations shall come, and say, Come, and let us go up to the mountain of the Lord, and to the house of the God of Jacob; and he will teach us of his ways, and we will walk in his paths: for the law shall go forth of Zion, and the word of the Lord from Jerusalem. And he shall judge among many people,*

CHAPTER TEN

and rebuke strong nations afar off; and they shall beat their swords into plowshares, and their spears into pruning hooks: nation shall not lift up a sword against nation, neither shall they learn war any more. But they shall sit every man under his vine and under his fig tree; and none shall make them afraid: for the mouth of the Lord of hosts hath spoken it.

From this portion of the Bible, we see we would become a point of attraction to the strong nations. Guilt would begin to run in their hearts, and they would turn their swords into ploughshares – meaning the money spent on war materials would be spent on agriculture, and we would have more food to eat. Aside of this, we would have more time to think about the future and plan for our children, including our unborn sons and daughters.

Throughout the days of King Solomon, he saw peace, and the land of Israel experienced the highest recognition that any land had ever seen. The wisdom of Solomon attracted all and sundry to the land of Israel, and the God of Israel became a God to be sought after, as a custodian of wisdom.

To be able to measure world peace and rank nations according to their peace profile, the Global Peace Index

CHAPTER TEN

(GPI) developed some 22 ranking criteria discussed earlier. Lending credence to our previous discussion, the online Wikipedia says: *in attempting to gauge peacefulness, the GPI investigates the extent to which countries are involved in ongoing domestic and international conflicts. It also seeks to evaluate the level of harmony or discord within a nation; ten indicators broadly assess what might be described as a safety and security in society. The assertion is that low crime rates, minimal incidences of terrorist acts and violent demonstrations, harmonious relations with neighbouring countries, a stable political scene and a small proportion of the population being internally displaced or refugees can be equated with peacefulness.*[xxix]

According to the GPI 2014 ranking figures, Iceland became the most peaceful nation, ranking as number 1, while Syria was the most warring nation with a ranking of 162. Nigeria was ranked 151 in the same year. From 2008 to 2014, Iceland had been on top of the list, while Syria dropped to the bottom of the list from 77 to 162, and Nigeria from 118 to 151. The United States of America has remained relatively stable on 100.

What is the special thing that Iceland had done that

CHAPTER TEN

has made it remain peaceful, that other nations haven't done? On further research, I found that Iceland has a small population, and is in geographical area with high volcanic activity, despite the nation having great economic affluence. It has had its own share of conflicts, but one thing I discovered as I read about Iceland on the Internet is that it is a nation that does not have much concern for religion differences, and could not be seen as a religious nation. Iceland is said to be a very secular country, and religious attendance is relatively low. It is ranked among the top 10 atheist populations in the world. However, 0.26% of the population is Islam, while 86.78% are Christians. The ratio of Islam to Christian would be 1 to 333 (1:333). In 2003, Iceland also supported the invasion of Iraq by deploying a Coast Guard EOD (Explosive Ordinance Disposal) team to Iraq. For the love of peace, Iceland hosted the historic 1986 Reagan–Gorbachev summit in Reykjavík, which set the stage for the end of the Cold War. Do these facts send a message about why the place is relatively peaceful? As a result of this, Iceland has the second highest quality of life in the world, according to the Economist Intelligence Index of 2011. Its strategic economic position in the world has earned it some form of military protection, first from the US and now from the Italian government[xxx].

This peace should last, as long as Iceland continues to occupy the strategic economic position of fish supplier to the world and does not allow the ratio of Islam to Christian to increase. The Global Peace Index reports that Iceland is the most peaceful country in the world, due to the fact that it does not have armed forces, experiences a low crime rate and has a high level of socio-political stability [31][xxxi]. This is possible when there is negligible inter-faith difference.

CHAPTER ELEVEN

HOW TO EMBRACE PEACE

Christ is the answer to world peace. The more I examine the life of Christ and the gospel of love and unity he preached and commanded us to live by, I see no other way of achieving world peace.

When David fled from King Saul in the cave, he wrote Psalm 57:

Be merciful unto me, O God, be merciful unto me: for my soul trusteth in thee: yea, in the shadow of thy wings will I make my refuge, until these calamities be overpast. I will cry unto God most high; unto God that performeth all things for me. He shall send from heaven, and save me from the reproach of him that would swallow me up. God shall send forth his mercy and his truth. My soul is among

CHAPTER ELEVEN

lions: and I lie even among them that are set on fire, even the sons of men, whose teeth are spears and arrows, and their tongue a sharp sword. Be thou exalted, O God, above the heavens; let thy glory be above all the earth. They have prepared a net for my steps; my soul is bowed down: they have digged a pit before me, into the midst whereof they are fallen themselves. My heart is fixed, O God, my heart is fixed: I will sing and give praise. Awake up, my glory; awake, psaltery and harp: I myself will awake early. I will praise thee, O Lord, among the people: I will sing unto thee among the nations. For thy mercy is great unto the heavens, and thy truth unto the clouds. Be thou exalted, O God, above the heavens: let thy glory be above all the earth.

If we read between the lines of the psalm above, we will begin to see the heart of an innocent one being hunted. David won a war that would have rendered Israel desolate, and out of jealousy, a King ordained by God is after His life, which means Saul would be using the ammunition of the nation to pursue a selfish interest. Is this not what has happened all around the globe, as political leaders, or militia leaders, for self-interest embark on the purchase of ammunitions, and then use drugs to inflict madness on those they would recruit to fight their course? Because of the high level of deprivation, people are willing to do all manner of assignments and jobs to put food on their tables.

Peace starts by coming to God, as David did above. We may see from Isaiah 1:18-20, that the Lord is inviting us to reason with Him, in what I would see as a peace talk: *Come now, and let us reason together, saith the Lord: though your sins be as scarlet, they shall be as white as snow; though they be red like crimson, they shall be as wool. If ye be willing and obedient, ye shall eat the good of the land: But if ye refuse and rebel, ye shall be devoured with the sword: for the mouth of the Lord hath spoken it.*

Like many nations worldwide, Nigeria has experienced various signs of desolation such as armed robbery, ritual killing, religious insurgence, militancy, kidnapping, increasing divorce, poor health care system, poor educational system, advance fee fraud, increasing confraternities, embezzlement and looting, aggressive wealth pursuit, drugs and human trafficking, etc. Economic and political interests have taken over our conscience for national growth and stability, causing disorientation to the pursuit of the goals of oneness. It could be argued that since Nigeria, which is today seen as an 'emerging market' by the World Bank, and being a former British protectorate, is suffering from the pains inflicted upon its soul by the colonial authorities.

The British presence in pre-independence Nigeria was the Royal Niger Company and with this the economy of the nation was seen as a piece of cake that would not be left 'undevoured.' I strongly believe that the attainment of independence was allowed with some reservations on the British side, with a strong loyalty from the Nigerian Government to the business interests of the British. The Lord was right when He said that the trouble the world is having is from the influence of the spirit of mammon – Luke 16:13: *Ye cannot serve God and mammon.*

Looking into the history of Nigeria reveals only one picture – the greed of the colonial masters. How did all this start? We are admonished thus:

- **Ephesians 4:22-24:** *That ye put off concerning the former conversation the old man, which is corrupt according to the deceitful lusts; And be renewed in the spirit of your mind; And that ye put on the new man, which after God is created in righteousness and true holiness.*

- **Galatians 5:26:** *Let us not be desirous of vainglory, provoking one another, envying one another.*

CHAPTER ELEVEN

The gospel of Christ is a call to freedom. The will of God for the world is that we have the opportunity, the power and the aspiration to exercise the gift of our salvation in Christ now and in the thousand years to come when the devil will be locked up – Revelation 20:7. We can make things right, if we can hold on to the word of God.

Many have asked me to tell them what sin is, so that they can avoid it and do the will of God, in a bid to experience peace. We see a clue to what we need to do from Revelation 9:20-21: *And the rest of the men which were not killed by these plagues yet repented not of the works of their hands, that they should not worship devils, and idols of gold, and silver, and brass, and stone, and of wood: which neither can see, nor hear, nor walk: Neither repented they of their murders, nor of their sorceries, nor of their fornication, nor of their thefts.*

So from here we would list what we must avoid to experience peace with the Lord:

- Worship of idols. An idol is anything that takes your love from God. It is mostly associated with the pursuit of money.
- Do not be associated with one who murders, and has bloodstains on their hands.

CHAPTER ELEVEN

- Do not practise witchcraft and sorcery.
- Flee fornication and adultery.
- Do not cheat or steal.

The wrath of God comes upon those who have not repented. We still have the time to repent, and today is the time. Let's do it now, and lay war to rest, so that peace can reign.

CHAPTER TWELVE

THE BOTTOM LINE

It is time to make peace; it is time to unite so that we can move forward. Walk up to your brother and say, 'I am sorry.' Walk up to your sister and say, 'I am sorry.' This is how to start reconciliation. There is really no reason for that quarrel, fighting or disagreement. Walk up to your spouse and say 'I am sorry.' We should drop our egos and seek peace. Jesus died for love. The Bible says in John 3:16: *For God so loved the world, that he gave his only begotten Son, that whosoever believeth in him should not perish, but have everlasting life. For God sent not his Son into the world to condemn the world; but that the world through him might be saved.*

If it works in the home, it will work elsewhere. Unity starts from the heart. What are you giving for love? Ask yourself this question. We can live together as one. We can stay together as one family and we can lean on each other's shoulders for help, if only we believe. If we truly believe we can live together, we can do so.

There is peace and unity in heaven. We should not allow the devil to pull at our hearts. We should drop our egos and pride right now. We need unity to live on earth, even as it is now in heaven after the devil was cast out of their midst. We can cast out the devil from our midst, from the government and all our institutions of decision-making, and we will see peace returning to us. There is no reason for Moslems fighting Christians, and there is no reason for Christians fighting Moslems – we are all children of the most High God. Let us exercise the law in heaven here on Earth. In the Lord's Prayer, He prayed – Matthew 6:10: *Thy kingdom come. Thy will be done in earth, as it is in heaven.* If we can do the will of God here on Earth, then we would experience peace as it is in Heaven. Jesus didn't came to start a religion, He came to establish the will of God in our hearts, so that we would have the wisdom and power to put things right. To Christ, there is nothing like Christianity, all He knows are those doing the will of the Father as He commanded. Using the name Christianity even denominates the purpose of God.

CHAPTER TWELVE

Jesus is not expecting mankind to belong to a sect or a denomination. All He sees is the salvation of the whole world – John 3:17: *For God sent not his Son into the world to condemn the world; but that the world through him might be saved.* This is why we bear the name 'Christ Movement'. We are doing the will of the Father, through Jesus Christ, who died to connect us to the vine of life. We can pray together as one, and seek the help of God in the affairs of the nations. The world is dying for the lack of love. We can make peace – it is within our reach and control. This was the advice of God to Cain, before he unleashed terror on his brother, and started the first spill of blood on the Earth – Genesis 4:7: *...sin lieth at the door. And unto thee shall be his desire, and thou shalt rule over him.* From this verse, we see that the Bible refers to the devil, and he acts in line with our command and instructions. Which imply that we can rule over evil if we desire it so - 2 Timothy 2:22-25: *... follow righteousness, faith, charity, peace, with them that call on the Lord out of a pure heart. But foolish and unlearned questions avoid, knowing that they do gender strifes. And the servant of the Lord must not strive; but be gentle unto all men, apt to teach, patient, In meekness instructing those that oppose*

CHAPTER TWELVE

themselves; if God peradventure will give them repentance to the acknowledging of the truth.

If we must have peace, then change is inevitable. If we look at society today, and all the atrocities that humans are committing, we would be, again, on the verge of praying for a messiah to come. So many times, people have asked, when will the world end? We have a duty and it starts now:

- Dedicate the country to God.
- Dedicate the land to God, that He would sanctify it for His use.
- Dedicate the atmosphere to God – let the angels embark on territorial control and seize it from satanic manipulations in high places.
- Cancel war and pestilence and proclaim peace upon the earth 7 times.
- Pray for infrastructural resuscitation in the country.
- Dedicate ourselves to the service of God.

God saves the righteous. We don't need to wage wars; God will deliver us if we follow His ways. We have a word of encouragement in Psalm 68:1-3: *Let God arise, let his enemies be scattered: let them also that hate him*

CHAPTER TWELVE

flee before him. As smoke is driven away, so drive them away: as wax melteth before the fire, so let the wicked perish at the presence of God. But let the righteous be glad; let them rejoice before God: yea, let them exceedingly rejoice.

Amen!

COVENANT CONFESSION

If you are not born again, you may have read this book as literary material and will not receive the spirit it carries. You can make a decision to correct that now by saying this covenant confession:

Lord Jesus, I know now that you died for my sins. I believe and confess you as my Lord and Saviour. Please come into my life and dwell inside me.

If you just said this confession, you should locate a spirit-filled church to fellowship with them – let the pastor know you just gave your life to Christ and you will be directed on what to do next. Salvation is a personal race and you must be serious about it.

You can also call us through the numbers below: +234-8076190064; +234-8086737791. Or send us an email at: christmovementinternational@gmail.com.

OTHER BOOKS BY THE SAME AUTHOR

1. Existing In The Supernatural
2. The Altar In Golgotha
3. How Good and Large is your Land?
4. Born To Blossom
5. Battles Beyond The Physical
6. The Path To Absolute Freedom
7. The Man God Made
8. Aspects of Marriage
9. Leadership – An Eagle-Eye Perspective
10. Gifted and Anointed
11. The Subject of Love – A Discourse
12. Mystery of the Kingdom of God on Earth
13. The Nonsense of War

ABOUT THE AUTHOR

Pastor Oghenethoja Umuteme encountered God the day he was baptised at the St Stephen's Anglican Church, Owhelogbo Delta State, when he received a warm feeling in his heart as he confessed the Lord Jesus as His lord and personal saviour. His birth was surrounded with mysteries – he was born to a mother who had been barren for 8 years.

There was hardly anything he said that did not come to pass as he was growing. In 1994 he had a dream in which he received an orange which contained a bible with a red cover. Events continued dramatically until he started hearing voices telling him to go for rescue, as many souls were heading for destruction. Then it became clear to him that he was being called to carry out the task of restoring mankind back to Jesus.

In January 2006, he heard a voice telling him to read Isaiah 42. On reading to verse 6, he felt a deep force within him and started trembling and a voice said - 'I have called you'. As he read further he was getting immersed in the spirit of God and when he read verse 22, the voice said, 'this is your task'. Then on the 13th of October 2008, he heard a voice while driving: 'Service starts in your house on Sunday.' Events happened that were beyond his understanding and on Sunday 19th October 2008, the first public worship service came to pass.

Pastor Oghenethoja Umuteme is a prolific writer and oversees a leadership foundation, Umuteme Leadership Foundation, which he uses to teach good leadership and a School of Ministry to empower church leaders. A member of the Nigerian Society of Engineers, he has eleven years' work experience in the oil and gas industry in different pipeline engineering functions – design, procurement, fabrication, construction, integrity management, maintenance and operation. Oghenethoja is a recipient of the Danish Institute for Human Rights Certificate.

A gospel songwriter and musician with two recorded albums, *Breaking Through* and *Smile Again*, he is also the Founder and Senior Pastor at Royal Diamonds International Church, Port Harcourt, Nigeria. He is an established teacher of the word of God and a prophet to the nation, as shown by his books. Using his crusade ministry – Giant Strides World Outreach Crusade - Pst. Oghenethoja reaches people with the undiluted word of salvation. And as a prophet to the nations, he has declared prophecies that have been fulfilled – the latest one being the famine that will visit the earth for ten years starting from the year 2017 and ending in 2027. He is also a man of miracles with testimonies said by those who have benefited from the gift of God in his life. As a motivational preacher, he has encouraged many to become successful in their chosen careers. The books God has used him to write has brought healing and encouraged many all over the world with testimonies. Many, including pastors, have also used these books as teaching and counselling materials. A time with him is a time filled with wisdom, joy and humour. He is often referred to as *'primus inter pares.'* His wife, Mrs. Umuteme Adokiye Obele, who supports him in this call of God upon his life, has borne him children – Elomezino, Aghoghomena and Ewevino.

REFERENCES

i   Andre de Guillaume. How To Rule The World – A Handbook of the Aspiring Dictator. USA. Chicago Review Press, Incorporated. 2003.

ii   Keegan, John. Interview granted to Booknotes. Retrieved 26th September, 2014, from http://www.booknotes.org

iii   http://en.wikipedia.org/wiki/Honorificabilitudinitatibus

iv   Peters, Ralph. New Glory: Expanding America's Global Supremacy, 2005. p. 30

v   Oghenethoja Umuteme. The Altar In Golgotha., 2010. p174. Nigeria: Ecnel printing Services.

vi   Casus Belli. Wikipedia. Retrieved 28th September 2014, from http://en.wikipedia.org/wiki/Casus_belli.

vii   Evans Andrews: 6 Wars Fought for Ridiculous Reasons. http://www.history.com/news/history-lists/6-wars-fought-for-ridiculous-reasons. Retrieved 28th September 2014.

viii   American Civil War. 2014. Encyclopædia Britannica Online. Retrieved 29 September, 2014, from http://www.britannica.com/EBchecked/topic/19407/American-Civil-War

ix   Spanish-American war. 2014. Retrieved 29th September 2014, from https://history.state.gov/milestones/1866-1898/spanish-american-war.

x   http://en.wikipedia.org/wiki/Causes_of_World_War_I. Retrieved 29th September, 2014

xi   http://www.bbc.com/news/magazine-26048324. Retrieved 29th of September 2014

xii   http://www.history.com/topics/world-war-ii. Retrieved 1st October 2014

xiii   Six-Day War. 2014. Encyclopædia Britannica Online. Retrieved 29 September, 2014, from http://www.britannica.com/EBchecked/topic/850855/Six-Day-War

xiv   Vietnam War. 2014. Encyclopædia Britannica Online. Retrieved 29 September, 2014, from http://www.britannica.com/EBchecked/topic/628478/Vietnam-War

xv   Major Abubakar A. Atofarati. The Nigerian Civil War, Causes, Strategies, And Lessons Learnt. Retrieved 30th September, 2014 from http://www.africamasterweb.com/BiafranWarCauses.html

xvi   http://en.wikipedia.org/wiki/Financial_cost_of_the_Iraq_War#cite_note-20

xvii   http://www.reuters.com/article/2013/03/14/us-iraq-war-anniversary-idUSBRE92D0PG20130314. Daniel Trotta, Reuters, 14 March 2013, accessed 18 March 2013

xviii   History of the British Empire. Boer War: 1899-1902. Retrieved 30th September, 2014, from http://www.historyworld.net/wrldhis/PlainTextHistories.asp?gtrack=pthc&ParagraphID=otl#otl#ixzz3EqHkFrDl

xix   "Cults of violence – How student fraternities turned into powerful and well-armed gangs". The Economist. 31 July 2008. Retrieved 7 June 2011.

xx   Information about indicators and methodology "2013 Global Peace Index". Institute for Economics and Peace. Retrieved 2013-06-24, from http://www.visionofhumanity.org/pdf/gpi/2013_Global_Peace_Index_Report.pdf

xxi   Oghenethoja Umuteme. Leadership – An Eagle Eye Perspective. England: Memoirs Publishing, 2012.

xxii   Wars Against children. UN report calls for action to protect children from armed conflict. Retrieved 1st October 2014 from http://www.unicef.org/graca/summry.htm

xxiii   Children Victims of War and Natural Disasters. Retrieved 2nd of October 2014, from http://www.unesco.org/new/en/social-and-human-sciences/themes/fight-against-discrimination/education-of-children-in-need/children-victims-of-war-and-natural-disasters/

xxiv   Jack Vance. Dying Earth. Retrieved on the 2nd of October 2014, from http://en.wikipedia.org/wiki/Dying_Earth

xxv History.com staff. Bombing of Hiroshima and Nagasaki. A+E Networks. Accessed 2nd October 2014, from http://www.history.com/topics/world-war-ii/bombing-of-hiroshima-and-nagasaki

xxvi AtmocBombMuseum.org. Retrieved 4th October 2014, from http://atomicbombmuseum.org/3_social.shtml

xxvii Martin J. Sherwin. A World Destroyed: Hiroshima and Its Legacies. USA: Stanford University Press; 1 edition (August 11, 2003) P91.

xxviii Ban Ki-moon, UN Secretary General. Remarks to the Conference on Disarmament. Geneva (Switzerland), 26 January 2011, Accessed 2nd October 2014, from http://www.un.org/sg/selected-speeches/statement_full.asp?statID=1055

xxix Global Peace Index. http://en.wikipedia.org/wiki/Global_Peace_Index#cite_note-1

xxx Iceland. Retrieved 4th October 2014, from http://en.wikipedia.org/wiki/Iceland

xxxi 2011 METHODOLOGY, RESULTS & FINDINGS. Institute for Economics and Peace (2011). visionofhumanity.org

www.ingramcontent.com/pod-product-compliance
Lightning Source LLC
Chambersburg PA
CBHW071703040426
42446CB00011B/1893